ANYONE
BUT ME

ANYONE
BUT ME

10 WAYS TO OVERCOME YOUR FEAR AND
BE PREPARED TO SHARE THE GOSPEL

RAY COMFORT

BakerBooks

a division of Baker Publishing Group
Grand Rapids, Michigan

Published by Baker Books
a division of Baker Publishing Group
PO Box 6287, Grand Rapids, MI 49516-6287
www.bakerbooks.com

Library of Congress Cataloging-in-Publication Data
Names: Comfort, Ray, author.
Title: Anyone but me : 10 ways to overcome your fear and be prepared to share the gospel / Ray Comfort.
Description: Grand Rapids, Michigan : Baker Books, a division of Baker Publishing Group, [2020] | Includes bibliographical references.
Identifiers: LCCN 2019035138 | ISBN 9780801093999 (paperback)
Subjects: LCSH: Courage—Religious aspects—Christianity. | Fear—Religious aspects—Christianity. | Witness bearing (Christianity)
Classification: LCC BV4647.C75 C66 2020 | DDC 248/.5—dc23
LC record available at https://lccn.loc.gov/2019035138

But sanctify the Lord God in your hearts, and always be ready to give a defense to everyone who asks you a reason for the hope that is in you, with meekness and fear.

1 Peter 3:15

Contents

ONE

Loving

Always Ready

And though I bestow all my goods to feed the poor, and though I give my body to be burned, but have not love, it profits me nothing.

1 Corinthians 13:3

"I make fun of people like you! Okay? I take idiotic extremists like you and make them look like a fool!"[1] These were the cutting words of high-profile atheist Jaclyn Glenn. It was back in 2013, just after she had seen our film *Evolution vs. God*. I had visited four evolutionary scientists at prestigious universities and pressed them on camera for *scientific* evidence for Darwinian evolution. They couldn't think of any, and they looked foolish.

Jaclyn made her own video and posted it on YouTube. She was serious and furious, and she directed her anger at me personally.

> Sometimes people like you deserve to be insulted. Sometimes people are *worthy* of being insulted in the worst possible way. And you at the top of the list, because you, sir, are certainly deserving of insult. You know what? You deserve worse than that in my opinion. You want to know why? Because you are so entirely #$@/!* that calling you stupid isn't good enough! You are a liar! *You* are a con man!

Then, in December 2017, she posted another video in which she said to her seven hundred thousand–plus subscribers:

> If you don't know who Ray Comfort is, he is Banana Man. That's Ray Comfort. He is the guy who made the documentary *Evolution vs. God* that I debunked. Now this was a long time ago, and because of that video I made—that actually got quite a bit of attention [over one million views]—Ray Comfort %#@&$! hates me.

After seeing the clip, I purchased a gift card, found out where she lived, mailed it to her, and forgot about it . . . until January 2018 when a friend directed me to another one of her videos. I found it and braced myself for another tirade. She said:

> I just went through my mail, and I got this letter. And this is one of the craziest things that I've ever gotten in my PO Box. About this particular letter . . . when I opened it up, my jaw hit the floor. And you guys are going to see what

I got in my mailbox that totally blew my mind. So I first of all open the package, and I see this—and it says "Living Waters" on it. And I know Living Waters, what that is, because that is the YouTube channel that Ray Comfort uses to post his videos—like for example, the one that I just reviewed: *Christmas Gone Viral.* You know Ray Comfort, Banana Man. He says that bananas are evidence for God, as I explained in my last video. So Living Waters is something I recognized. This person sent me a $100 gift card, which is a lot of money; so I was surprised when I looked at this letter. It's a very short letter, but it says, "Jaclyn, from Ray and Sue Comfort. PS saw your review of Christmas Gone Viral. BTW I don't hate you ☺."

I'm not even kidding. I don't think that this is a joke. I think this is *really* him, and that's amazing, if he doesn't really hate me. I think that is amazing, because I have not been censored, or I haven't been gentle in going after some of the things he has posted on the internet. But if he wants to be friends . . . Ray Comfort, if you're watching this, I would totally make a video with you. If you were interested in an interview or a kind of just silly video, saying hello; it doesn't have to be anything too crazy, just have to be something we can both agree on. If you aren't uncomfortable, I would totally make a video with you. *But this just blew my mind.* I can't believe that I got a freaking card, a gift card too—from Ray Comfort. And he saw my video review. That made my day. I don't know if you people understand the gravity of this for me. I have been feuding with Ray Comfort for like, four years. Like the first thing I made against him was like forever ago, and then he made a video back at me and then it was this crazy thing. So for this to happen now, after all of this time . . . I am super excited about it.

As I watched Jaclyn's reaction, *I* was the one who was blown away. Her comments were all because I had sent her a gift card. Christians are always ready to show love and kindness to each other. We give gift cards to each other without a second thought. It's not even unusual for a Christian to give another Christian a car. Our nonprofit ministry, Living Waters, often gets generous, unsolicited financial gifts to support our ministry, and we send gifts to other ministries. That's just the way it is within the body of Christ. Scripture says, "And let us not grow weary while doing good, for in due season we shall reap if we do not lose heart. Therefore, as we have opportunity, let us do good to all, especially to those who are of the household of faith" (Gal. 6:9–10).

We focus on "especially to those who are of the household of faith" and run with it. We often overlook "let us do good to all." Giving to others is the outward expression of the indwelling love of God. It's easy.

But the atheist world isn't like ours. It is a barren, dark desert of selfishness. *Any* acts of love and kindness from the hand of a Christian stand out. For Jaclyn, that small gift was a big bright light that burst into her dark world, and it came close to bringing her to tears.

Look at what some other Scripture passages say about Christians doing good to others—whether or not those others are Christians.

> Now may our Lord Jesus Christ Himself, and our God and Father, who has loved us and given us everlasting consolation and good hope by grace, comfort your hearts *and establish*

you in every good word and work. (2 Thess. 2:16–17, emphasis added)

Paul's prayer is that those in the Thessalonian church would be *established* by God *in every good work.* Later in the same letter, he writes, "But as for you, brethren, *do not grow weary in doing good*" (3:13, emphasis added).

In all things showing yourself to be a *pattern* of good works; in doctrine showing integrity, reverence, incorruptibility, sound speech that cannot be condemned, *that one who is an opponent* may be ashamed, having nothing evil to say of you. (Titus 2:7–8, emphasis added)

Our pattern of good works confounds the *unsaved* who oppose us. They will be ashamed and have nothing evil to say about us. Paul is not referring to giving money to our church or a Christian organization secretly—but it's true that we are not to let our left hand know what our right hand is doing within the body of Christ. These good works aren't an effort to earn points with God or to make us look holier than thou. God forbid. If I ever do any good, I want it to be known that I'm not boasting of personal virtue.

When I do something nice for an unsaved person, I am saying, "I love you. But I have another motive too. I desperately want to bring you to the cross so that you will escape hell. That's my deepest desire." Our aim is love, welling up from a pure motive: "Now the purpose of the commandment is love from a pure heart, from a good conscience, and from sincere faith" (1 Tim. 1:5).

The Christian life should be an established pattern of good works, a lifestyle of *doing good that can be seen by the ungodly—to the end, their eternal salvation.*

The video Jaclyn Glenn made about my gift card received over 120,000 views, and here are just a few of the more than one thousand comments:

> Well I'll be d***ed. That's legitimately nice. Never thought I'd say this but good on you, Ray Comfort. DG

> Ray Comfort sent a fruit basket to Hugo and Jake from *The Bible Reloaded* after Life Water flagged their #@!% as an apology, so I wouldn't doubt the legitimacy of your gift. He seems like a nice guy in spite of his #@!% beliefs. JG

> While I don't agree w/Ray Comfort, I've heard that he's a pretty nice guy . . . (He's still wrong, though). P

> A lovely example of the phrase "Love thy neighbor." The only phrase from religious text which I agree with. JJ

> That's really actually cool of Ray. CK

> Wow. You got free money from one of the dumbest people on the planet. SB

I can't repeat the disgusting language normally used by atheists to describe me, but this gift turned me from Hitler to Mother Theresa in a moment of time. I'm not a nice guy at all. Rather, this is what happened: "For this is the will of God, that by doing good you may put to silence the ignorance of foolish [people]" (1 Pet. 2:15).

It was part of a pattern of good works that we do so that those who are opposed may be ashamed, having nothing evil to say of us.

Those Who Have Ears

I love the words Jesus used to precede the command to love our enemies. He said that what He was about to say was *for those who could hear Him*. It was for those slaves of Christ whose ear had been fastened to the Door (see John 10:9; Exod. 21:5–6). Jesus said to those who were truly His disciples: "But I say *to you who hear*: Love your enemies, do good to those who hate you" (Luke 6:27, emphasis added).

Do you *hear* what Jesus is saying? Can you see the faith, the wisdom, the effort, and the obedience that it takes for you and me to love our enemies? Our unconditional love sets Christians apart from the world and stops the ignorant mouths of evil men. Loving enemies is a light that glorifies God.

Stephen loved his enemies, even though it cost him his life. His faithfulness to the gospel stirred hateful demons that frothed at the mouth and shed his blood. He stepped onto a bed of rattlesnakes—that is, he infuriated the religious leaders of his day.

Let's talk about religious leaders for a minute, so we know what Stephen was up against—because we're up against it too. John the Baptist's words help us understand: "But when he saw many of the Pharisees and Sadducees coming to his baptism, he said to them, 'Brood of vipers! Who warned you to flee from the wrath to come?'" (Matt. 3:7).

Jesus said to the religious leaders, "Serpents, brood of vipers! How can you escape the condemnation of hell?" (Matt. 23:33).

When we deal with the "religious"—those whose worldview is steeped in self-righteousness and rooted in idolatry—we are dealing with those who would kill us while thinking they were doing God a service (see John 16:2). We are stepping on rattlesnakes. My nastiest opponents to the gospel are those who profess to speak for God but who disbelieve the Bible. They have a form of godliness, they give lip service, but with it comes the devilish wisdom from below (see James 3:15). In speaking of human nature, Scripture says:

> Their throat is an open tomb;
> With their tongues they have practiced deceit;
> The poison of asps is under their lips. (Rom. 3:13)

Never forget that when you are dealing with snakes, they can turn on you in a second. As the religious leaders struck out at Stephen with deadly force, love poured from his lips: "And they stoned Stephen as he was calling on God and saying, 'Lord Jesus, receive my spirit.' Then he knelt down and cried out with a loud voice, 'Lord, do not charge them with this sin.' And when he had said this, he fell asleep" (Acts 7:59–60).

Love also filled his heart in his earlier words, though they were words that cut his hearers to the heart. It was love that quelled Stephen's fears when he said to them:

> You stiff-necked and uncircumcised in heart and ears! You always resist the Holy Spirit; as your fathers did, so do you.

Which of the prophets did your fathers not persecute? And they killed those who foretold the coming of the Just One, of whom you now have become the betrayers and murderers, who have received the law by the direction of angels and have not kept it. (vv. 51–53)

If open rebuke is better than secret love (see Prov. 27:5), how much better is a *loving* rebuke that has our hearers' eternal salvation in mind? They had not kept God's law, and Stephen told them so.

Stephen was a man filled with faith and the Holy Spirit (see Acts 6:5). The love of Christ compelled him to speak "the truth in love" (Eph. 4:15) because he loved his hate-filled hearers. Paul told Timothy to reprove and rebuke with all patience and doctrine (see 2 Tim. 4:2). That was Stephen's mission and motive, and it should be ours when we reprove stubborn sinners for violating that same law.

Whether they fall down on their knees in contrition for their sins or—like Stephen's hearers—are cut to the heart and gnash on us with their teeth like mad dogs, love them unconditionally. Love them because we are *commanded* to love our enemies. Love them because it is a witness that glorifies God. And who knows, in their midst may be a lone bystander: "Then they cried out with a loud voice, stopped their ears, and ran at him with one accord; and they cast him out of the city and stoned him. And the witnesses laid down their clothes at the feet of a young man named Saul" (7:57–58).

Stephen witnessed to Saul by dying. Saul became Paul and wrote half of the New Testament. You don't know who is standing on the sidelines of your own testimonies, so always witness boldly, even when things are going south.

So What?

Look at the word *so* in the following verse: "Let your light so shine before [others], that they may see your good works and glorify your Father in heaven" (Matt. 5:16).

The word *so* indicates *this is the reason* you should let your light shine before others: that they may *see* your good works and glorify God—not you.

There are many other admonitions for us to "do good to all" so that by doing so we may "put to silence the ignorance of foolish people" (the unsaved), which leaves us with the question, How do we practically do that? How can the average Christian have an established *pattern* of good works that is *seen* by the ungodly?

I have found an effective way.

Since 2016, I have given away $5 Subway gift cards after I share the gospel. This habit began after I heard that thousands of atheists were meeting in Washington, DC, for what they called a "Reason Rally." Atheists normally don't have a real reason to exist. They believe they are products of a random explosion in space, caused by nothing and for no reason. But I guess they thought of a reason. I decided to take a camera crew and film a couple of episodes of season five of our television program *Way of the Master*. This rally was a unique opportunity to show atheists that we loved them, so we purchased $25,000 worth of Subway cards to give to those who were attending the rally.

When we applied for a film permit, the DC police asked how many would be attending the shoot. About a thousand Christians had committed to help us film and give out cards. But the police decided that the last thing they wanted was violence breaking out between "religious extremists" and atheists, and they told us that if we approached any atheists we would be arrested.

I ended up with $25,000 worth of Subway cards in my pocket, most of which were given to the homeless in Los Angeles. However, a thousand or so were left over, and I began giving them to anyone with whom I shared the gospel.

Giving someone a gift card for no obvious reason was my way of saying, "Here's proof that I *really* care about you." It added *evidential* love to my witness. The person I spoke to may not have been convinced of the truth of the gospel, but I hoped they would think about what I said when they took the card to Subway and ate their free lunch. These small cards have become my big way of expressing unconditional love.

Giving People a Lift

A friend and I stepped into an elevator in a parking building after a day of open-air preaching in Huntington Beach. Two men who were obviously a couple stepped in with us. I handed one of them one of our movie gift cards (which point people to FullyFreeFilms.com)[2] and said, "Hello. Do you like free movies? We've produced eight movies. Six are award-winning, and they all are completely free."

We arrived on the first floor and the doors opened. As one of the men began moving forward, I held out a Subway card, saying, "And here's dinner for you and your friend."

He was taken aback and said, "Thank you." Then they were gone. A few minutes later, we prayed for both men and trusted God that they would be moved to watch the movies because of our small but evident token of love.

That cost me ten dollars. Perhaps you are thinking that you couldn't afford to do that every day—that's seventy dollars a week! I wouldn't consider myself to be wealthy, but here's the way I look at it: I can afford to be generous because I don't have a hobby or play a sport or belong to a fitness club.

Don't get me wrong. I enjoy sports and watching golf on TV, but by not being part of a club, I save money: "In 2008 *Golf Digest* surveyed more than 200 private-club members . . . [and] found that the average annual cost of a golf club membership was $6,240, or about $520 per month. Newer data doesn't show much change."[3]

How much is your hobby or sport costing you? Maybe you don't need to play so much. Could you give some of that monthly money away in the form of five dollar gift cards to unsaved people you witness to? Where else is your money going? Maybe you spend money on sodas or bottled water, or you're paying five dollars for a fancy cup of coffee you could have made yourself for about twenty cents. Perhaps you're going to nice restaurants instead of eating at home.

How do you create opportunities to show unconditional love? Here is my challenge to you: limit your spending and open a benevolence bank account for the money you save. Use that money to pay for some tokens of evident love. This is part of denying ourselves legitimate pleasures and taking up our cross daily (see Luke 9:23). But I have to say that I don't consider doing this a denial. It is a great joy to see unsaved people react to love. Almost every day I get to see reactions like Jaclyn Glenn's up close and personal. Seeing unsaved people moved by love is nothing short of a delight. Doing this daily also helps me to be free from the subtlety of the love of money (see Matt. 6:24).

You and I aren't the first ones to be challenged when it comes to giving our abundance back to God. When the apostle Paul wrote to the church in Corinth about giving a financial gift, he said:

> Therefore I thought it necessary to exhort the brethren to go to you ahead of time, and prepare your generous gift beforehand, which you had previously promised, that it may be ready as a matter of generosity and not as a grudging obligation.
>
> But this I say: He who sows sparingly will also reap sparingly, and he who sows bountifully will also reap bountifully. So let each one give as he purposes in his heart, not grudgingly or of necessity; for God loves a cheerful giver. And God is able to make all grace abound toward you, that you, always having all sufficiency in all things, may have an abundance for every good work. As it is written:
>
> "He has dispersed abroad,
> He has given to the poor;
> His righteousness endures forever." (2 Cor. 9:5–9)

Paul outlines the three stages of giving: grudgingly, out of necessity, cheerfully. I don't know about you, but I go through a wrestling match almost every time I have a conviction to give money to someone or to some cause. At first, I don't want to (grudgingly). Then I yield to what I feel I should do (out of necessity). Then I give cheerfully. What happens when *you* feel the call to give?

Get Out of Here!

I want to end the chapter on loving with an incident I found so moving, I couldn't relate it to anyone for days because my voice would crack and tears would come to my eyes.

I approached two young men who were sitting at a table in a park and politely asked, "Would you like to do an interview for YouTube?" In retrospect, they may have been dealing drugs.

The man on the left immediately responded, "Get out of here!" He raised his voice and repeated, "I said, *get out of here!*"

I looked at the man on the right and asked, "May I give you a gift?"

He calmly replied, "Sure."

"Here's a gift card for dinner tonight for you, and here's one for your friend."

As I turned to walk away, I heard a sound I'll never forget. It was a deep groan from the angry man on the left. "I'm *so* sorry," I heard him say.

I replied, "That's okay" (without looking back) as I walked away.

Evidential love has the power to immediately dissipate anger. If you share your faith, you will undoubtedly come across some angry responses. Most Christians don't realize that humanity hates the God of the Bible. Sinners don't hate *their own concept* of God as a father figure, friend, or divine butler.

The Scriptures say that before we came to Jesus, we were enemies of God in our minds through wicked works (see Col. 1:21) and that our minds were in a state of enmity with God (see Rom. 8:7). We were friends with the world and therefore enemies of God (see James 4:4). There is no greater example of contempt and hatred toward somebody than to use their name as a cuss word. Such is the contention between humanity and the one real God.

But when contentious sinners suddenly see their own selfish sins, then the *evidential* love displayed on the cross, they let out a deep groan. And from there, they are able to find a place of "godly sorrow [that] produces repentance" (2 Cor. 7:10). Biblical repentance is a change of mind about God and sin, which is evidenced by a change of direction—away from sin. The Bible says, "Let everyone who names the name of Christ *depart* from iniquity" (2 Tim. 2:19, emphasis added).

That is why we must preach Sinai before we preach Calvary. We preach Moses before we preach Jesus. The moral law must precede grace and bring the knowledge of sin, as we see happening in the case of Jesus and the rich young ruler (see Mark 10:17–18). The darkness of the law makes the light of the glorious gospel shine.

God's unconditional love is hidden from the world. But when it is seen, it is the light that shines in our hearts, glorifies God, and at the same time exalts the Savior:

But even if our gospel is veiled, it is veiled to those who are perishing, whose minds the god of this age has blinded, who do not believe, lest the light of the gospel of the glory of Christ, who is the image of God, should shine on them. For we do not preach ourselves, but Christ Jesus the Lord, and ourselves your bondservants for Jesus' sake. For it is the God who commanded light to shine out of darkness, who has shone in our hearts to give the light of the knowledge of the glory of God in the face of Jesus Christ. (2 Cor. 4:3–6)

Only when a sinner sees their sin can they truly see the Savior, and it's on that bloodstained cross that they will see the expressed love of God. Jesus Christ was *evidently* set forth and crucified (see Gal. 3:1). They see God *commending* His love for us while we are yet sinners. Only this will dissipate the enmity between humankind and God—in a moment of time.

If you have a bad witnessing experience, if someone rejects you because you are a Christian, rejoice. Rejoice because you've been told to rejoice. Rejoice because of the truth of Romans 8:28. Good can come out of something bad. Sweetness can come from the lion (see Judg. 14:14). Jesus has a way of turning the tables on moneychangers. That horrible experience of being rejected that day at the park became one of the most precious and unforgettable moments of my life. It continually reminds me of the power of unconditional love and motivates me to witness.

The love for unsaved people that God has given me is the foundation for my readiness—and willingness—to share the gospel. As I go through the nine additional qualities you need to be both an effective evangelist and effective in evangelism, remember that unconditional love is the base. If you find you are hesitant to share the gospel, thinking *anyone but me*, check in with your understanding of God's unconditional love for you. Do you believe in the power of the gospel? Remember, you were once unsaved. Someone was willing to share the gospel with you.

I can't emphasize enough the biblical truth that we don't wrestle against flesh and blood (see Eph. 6:12–20). Our battle is against an unseen enemy who will continually try to feed us propaganda. If you listen to his lies about you being unworthy, unequipped, unintelligent, unhinged, and unprepared, it will undermine your efforts to understand evangelism. You don't need much to plant seed because the quality is in the seed, not the sower. And that's all we are doing—planting precious seed. Just tell the underworld that you are both uninterested and underwhelmed and that what they are saying is unmistakably unwanted. Slam the door on the lies, and lock it.

All right. Let's dive in and consider more characteristics you need to be ready to share about the love of God.

TWO

Obedient

Samson's Secret Strength

Finally, my brethren, be strong in the Lord and in the power of His might.

Ephesians 6:10

Ephesians 6:10 is the final instruction from the apostle Paul to the troops before they head into battle. *Finally* is more than the merciful word we hear from the pulpit near the end of a long sermon. The word *finally* in this verse is an important military *summation*. It is saying, "What you are going to now hear is of vital importance."

The apostle is saying to hold on to every word because a soldier's strong mental attitude is more important than his physical weapons. Be *strong* in the Lord.

If anyone was strong, it was Samson. His name is synonymous with strength. His life is filled with hidden pictures of the ultimate strong One. For example, we're told that Samson defeated a lion with his bare hands: "And the Spirit of the LORD came mightily upon him, and he tore the lion apart as one would have torn apart a young goat, though he had nothing in his hand" (Judg. 14:6).

Jesus alone, however, conquered the fearsome lion of death. Humanity stood helpless and hopeless before its terrible jaws. Satan walked unhindered as a roaring lion, seeking whom he may devour. The god of this world once held the keys to death and hell, but through the cross and the resurrection, Jesus ripped them from his ugly hands (see Rev. 1:18). Look at how the *Amplified Bible* describes this:

> Therefore, since [these His] children share in flesh and blood [the physical nature of (hu)mankind], He Himself in a similar manner also shared in the same [physical nature, but without sin], so that through [experiencing] death He might make powerless (ineffective, impotent) him who had the power of death—that is, the devil—and [that He] might free all those who through [the haunting] fear of death were held in slavery throughout their lives. (Heb. 2:14–15)

Samson's strength wasn't in his hair. The root of his strength was his obedience to God. His human frailties disappeared when "the Spirit of the LORD came mightily upon him." Obedience was the secret to his power, and obedience is how you and I can overcome the frailties of our human nature.

The reason the apostle Paul tells us to be strong "in the Lord" is because *in the Lord* we have power and strength. The moment we are born again, the Spirit of the Lord doesn't only come upon us, as happened with Samson, but also *lives within* us. We are in the Lord, *He* is in us, and we can do what we need to do through Christ: "I can do all things through Christ who strengthens me" (Phil. 4:13).

When the Holy Spirit was given on the day of Pentecost, it was for the purpose of being witnesses of Christ. Jesus told His disciples: "But you shall receive power when the Holy Spirit has come upon you; and you shall be witnesses to Me in Jerusalem, and in all Judea and Samaria, and to the end of the earth" (Acts 1:8).

He came upon them and made His dwelling place within them. This wasn't temporary. It was *permanent*. He will never leave us nor forsake us: "If you love Me, keep My commandments. And I will pray the Father, and He will give you another Helper, *that He may abide with you forever*— the Spirit of truth, whom the world cannot receive, because it neither sees Him nor knows Him; but you know Him, for He dwells with you and will be in you" (John 14:15–17, emphasis added).

That means we *always* have access to the power of God and can always be ready. We have the same strength that Samson had. His was physical; ours is mental. We are to be strong—that is, obedient—*in the Lord*.

Let's take a look at the Greek to better understand the power and strength we have.

The Greek *dunamis* is used 120 times in the New Testament. Loosely, the word refers to "strength, power, or ability." It is the root word of our English words *dynamite*, *dynamo* and *dynamic*. . . .

In Matthew 22:29 Jesus tells the Sadducees, "You are in error because you do not know the Scriptures or the *power* of God." Jesus also said, "Then will appear the sign of the Son of Man in heaven. And then all the peoples of the earth will mourn when they see the Son of Man coming on the clouds of heaven, with *power* and great glory" (Matt. 24:30). In other words, the Lord has inherent power residing in Himself. *Dunamis* is part of His nature.[1]

In other words, the *strength* of almighty God Himself abides in the believer. *Do you believe that?* The Bible says, "But if the Spirit of Him who raised Jesus from the dead dwells in you, He who raised Christ from the dead will also give life to your mortal bodies through His Spirit who dwells in you" (Rom. 8:11).

Do you *really* believe that the same power that created this universe from nothing and raised Jesus from the dead dwells in you? Or do we cringe at the thought, in a false sense of humility? But if we *do* believe it, it should be evidenced by our confidence. We should be a powerful Samson in our convictions. We should have a *strong* mental attitude that is fueled by faith in God.

David and Goliath

Do other biblical heroes come to mind when you think of strength? David comes to mine. It wasn't *God* who ran at Goliath. It was *David*. And the mental attitude that fed the courage that caused him to *run* at the enemy was faith in God. David's faith made him bigger than Goliath. He was strong in the Lord.

Here's a question that will test our strength. Do we truly believe that if a sinner dies in their sins, they will go to a literal hell? We *must* if we are followers of Jesus Christ. He didn't lie about the existence of hell, and if we have the love of Christ in us, we will be deeply sober about his words: "Whatever I tell you in the dark, speak in the light; and what you hear in the ear, preach on the housetops. And do not fear those who kill the body but cannot kill the soul. But rather fear Him who is able to destroy both soul and body in hell" (Matt. 10:27–28).

Do you see what He is saying? He is telling His disciples that the world will not like what they are going to preach. He is telling them that they will have to be strong in their faith in order to obey His command. The world will try to suppress the truth and keep it in the dark, but they were to stubbornly preach it in the light. The world will try to keep us quiet too, but Jesus is saying to get *above* them and preach from the rooftops. We have a higher calling than the world.

Look at the strong mental attitude of the disciples after they were threatened not to preach any longer in the name of Jesus:

Why did the nations rage,
And the people plot [in] vain? . . .

For truly against Your holy Servant Jesus, whom You anointed, both Herod and Pontius Pilate, with the Gentiles and the people of Israel, were gathered together to do whatever Your hand and Your purpose determined before to be done. Now, Lord, look on their threats, and grant to Your servants that with all boldness they may speak Your word, by stretching out Your hand to heal, and that signs and wonders may be done through the name of Your holy Servant Jesus. (Acts 4:25–30)

They didn't back down. They *ran* at Goliath because they trusted God and knew that their calling was higher: "And when they had prayed, the place where they were assembled together was shaken; and they were all filled with the Holy Spirit, and they spoke the word of God with boldness" (v. 31).

Strength will come easily if we believe God's Word about the reality of the coming day of judgment. If an unsaved person dies in their sins, they will be damned in hell. What sort of hard-hearted, inhumane beast would I be if I was not grieved beyond words at such a thought?

The contemporary church doesn't seem to believe what the Bible says about hell. So the church needs an earthquake. It needs to be shaken out of its complacency. Judgment begins at the house of God (see 1 Pet. 4:17). Historically, this comes in the form of persecution. In the book of Acts, when complacency entered the church, Saul of Tarsus began a terrible persecution against the believers.

At that time a great persecution arose against the church which was at Jerusalem; and they were all scattered throughout the regions of Judea and Samaria, except the apostles. And devout men carried Stephen to his burial, and made great lamentation over him.

As for Saul, he made havoc of the church, entering every house, and dragging off men and women, committing them to prison.

Therefore those who were scattered went everywhere preaching the word. (Acts 8:1–4, emphasis added)

It took the chastening hand of persecution to stir the church to obedience to the Great Commission. We need the same momentum now. And in our obedience, we will find God to be strong.

Would We Tell Them?

What does obedience in strength look like in our daily lives? It starts with responding to our obligations. If a family climbed into a car that had faulty brakes, and we knew they would be going down a steep, winding road minutes after they left, would we tell them? *Of course we would.* How could we not? We are morally and legally obligated to say something because their lives are in our hands. We would plead with them, and no one could talk us out of warning them by saying they might think we're crazy. We will not hesitate for a second *if we believe what we are saying is true*—they are going to die if not stopped! Love would be strong, bulldog-persuasive, and deeply passionate.

Do we have the same conviction to warn sinners their brakes are faulty and they are going to fall headlong into hell? Are we mentally *strong* for the gospel? If we are "in the Lord," we will be, and the measure of our conviction will be in direct proportion to our love for the lost.

One of the greatest tests of my love happens when sinners hold on to false hope. They sit in the car and say that the brakes are okay; they will work, even though they are broken beyond repair. They admit to lying, stealing, lust, and blasphemy. I share the cross and the necessity of repentance and faith in Jesus, and they say, "I believe you. I pray every day. I know the Lord. I've been born again." Yet I know by the words that come out of their mouths that something is terribly wrong. I can either leave them in eternal danger or love them and tell them the truth. But can I be obedient without giving offense? There is a way.

First, I must have a basis for believing that this person is deceived. To do this, I look to a Bible verse that I've locked into my memory and can easily recall by thinking, *It's as easy as 1, 2, 3, and 4.* That reminds me of 1 John 2:3–4: "We know that we have come to know him if we keep his commands. Whoever says, 'I know him,' but does not do what he commands is a liar, and the truth is not in that person" (NIV).

If you are speaking to someone who is deceived into thinking all is right between them and God, quote these verses. Tell them that you are deeply concerned about their eternal salvation and that you love them enough to tell them the truth.

I'd continue the conversation with this illustration: "If you saw someone about to jump ten thousand feet out of a plane and their parachute straps were loose, would you tell them? Of course you would."

And then I say that I believe his straps need to be tightened up in his walk with the Lord. Almost always, those I speak to in this way detect my motive as being a loving concern *because of the tone of my voice.* Make sure your tone is loving. It should come naturally if you have a strong concern for that person's salvation.

Dog Evangelism

Expressing strength through obedience to the Great Commission can also be great fun. I had been taking my dog, Sam, on a bike ride twice a day for about eight months. The dog-on-bike daily excursion began when I once scooped Sam into my arms after he became tired while running beside me. He so enjoyed the ride, I built him a platform on my bike. Then I did something that changed my life. I got him a pair of sunglasses that matched mine.

The first time I took him for a ride, people came out of their homes and took photos, drivers honked their horns, and strangers waved, yelled out, smiled, and gave me the thumbs-up. Ever since then, strangers have approached me to chat about Sam. It suddenly became an incredible way to share the gospel. There is something disarming about a guy and a dog wearing sunglasses.

Every day, once in the morning and once in the afternoon, Sam and I would go witnessing and film the interview. Then my production team would put the clip on YouTube. When we announced we would post two new exciting clips every day, our Living Waters channel exploded, jumping to over sixty-six million views (and growing) by the end of 2018. Everyone, including Sam and me, loves dog evangelism!

Just after Christmas 2018, Sam and I were biking up a curved path that went around the local courthouse. I was chatting to him as we went down the other side. It didn't worry me that someone might hear me because they would probably think I was on a phone. I said something like "Sam, I really love this" as we rode downhill with green grass on each side of us. Suddenly, my heart sank. About sixty feet in front of me was a police officer, walking directly toward us. At that very second, my eye caught a sign that read, "No skateboarding, no bicycling. . . ." I was breaking the law and had been caught red-handed—outside of the courthouse. He looked directly at me, smiled from ear to ear, and said, "That's *so* cool!"

Two days later, I was at the local park, looking for strangers to interview. As we rode along the sidewalk, my heart sank again. A police car had driven up onto the sidewalk and was heading straight for me. I thought they were going to cite me and tell me to ride my bike on the road. The officer in the driver's seat said through the open window, "May we take a photo of your dog?"

Then the other officer said, "And can I ride your bike?"

I replied, "If you let me film you filming my dog." They said it was a deal, and I filmed one of the officers filming his buddy riding my bike with Sam.

It was a wonderful sight. Then both officers began to ask me why my dog was wearing sunglasses. I told them it was so that I could meet strangers and talk to them about the afterlife for our YouTube channel. They began to question me about salvation. Both officers thought they were good people, but when I took them through the Ten Commandments, they admitted to lying, blasphemy, and lusting after women. They denied that they had stolen anything, which is understandable for police officers. I didn't push it, because they should have been questioning me, not the other way around! They were Roman Catholics who had no idea why Jesus died on the cross. I spent fifteen to twenty minutes going through the law and the gospel with them. They were polite, humble, and very thankful, and each took a "Hell's Best Kept Secret" CD, a movie gift card, Million Dollar Bill tracts, and a signed copy of *How to Battle Depression and Suicidal Thoughts* (republished under the title, *The Final Curtain*). So don't tell me that obedience is never fun—you'll have to answer to a dog in sunglasses.

Are You Over Eighteen?

Don't think you won't feel nervous when you're trying your best to obey. I'm always a little apprehensive when I approach a stranger to ask if they would like to be on camera for our YouTube channel.

Once, when I was approaching a parked car, I was a little more apprehensive than usual as I couldn't see the driver's face.

I said, "Hello, would you like to be interviewed for our YouTube channel?" When he looked up, I saw a rather startled young face and added, "Are you over eighteen?" When he said he wasn't, I told him that California law required people to be over eighteen to be interviewed. Then I said, "Nice to meet you," and rode away on my bike.

Suddenly, I had an overwhelming concern for his salvation. If I had the love of God in my heart, I *couldn't* ride away. I did a U-turn, went back, and asked, "What's your name?"

The young man looked even more startled and asked, "Why?"

I jokingly told him that *Why* was an unusual name. Then I asked him what he thought happened when somebody died.

He seemed a little uncomfortable and said that he didn't know—that his father was a Catholic and his mother was a Jehovah's Witness. I asked him if that left him confused.

For the first time in our conversation he smiled slightly. That was my opening to explain to him how biblical Christianity is different.

Both Jehovah's Witnesses and the Catholic Church teach *works righteousness* salvation—that is, they will say they are saved by grace, but they have to *do* something to *merit* everlasting life. The thing that separates us from the notion that salvation can be earned is the law of God. It reveals that we are criminals before a morally perfect Judge, and *anything* we offer Him is an attempt to bribe Him to pervert justice. I then asked if he thought he was a good person and took him through some of the Ten Commandments to show him that there was no way any of us could *earn* everlasting life. I shared the mercy of God in Christ—that God Himself made the way of salvation through the cross.

Why was very grateful and explained in an apologetic way why he answered "Why?" when I asked for his name. He was smoking marijuana while having a bite of lunch. Suddenly, I showed up at his car window, and he thought I was an undercover cop. I was wearing the standard-looking police officer sunglasses and asking for his name, his age, and *what he thought happened when someone died.* That last one sounded a little like a threat.

As I rode away, this thought struck me: every Christian is an undercover law officer. We are representatives of God and His law, and *that* law is much scarier.

The Duke

Two days later, I had another witnessing experience that proves we can be strong and obedient even under awkward circumstances. My wife, Sue, wanted to go shopping, and I decided to go with her but to stay in the car and write. I grabbed my dog, my iPad, my iPhone, and a couple of copies of my books to stash in the glove box and hopped into the passenger seat.

Sue had been away for about twenty minutes when a gentleman parked his car alongside ours. I was sitting in the passenger seat, so I lowered the driver's side window and reached across to give him one of our Million Dollar Bill gospel tracts as he stood by his car. He smiled as he looked at it, then noticed Sam and said, "What an *adorable* dog!" That was an unusual choice of words. Men in their late forties wearing cowboy hats don't generally use words like *adorable*. Those who do are true-blue dog lovers. This man was. He had two canines that he adored, and so for the next couple of minutes we talked about dogs.

Then I leaned across the driver's seat and shook hands with him as we introduced ourselves.

I asked, "Duke, do you think there's an afterlife?" This is a question that opens doors without offense because it doesn't mention Jesus, God, sin, the Bible, Heaven, or hell. It simply asks for an opinion. This question helps me to run at Goliath. It's an unassuming but powerful weapon that helps me to be strong in obedience.

Duke said he sure did. When I asked if he was a Christian, he said he believed but wasn't living the life. Here was a test of the depth of my obedience. I could have said, "Duke, you're a believer. That's great! God bless you, sir. It was great to meet you." But I couldn't. Obedience wouldn't let me.

I suspected that he hadn't seen his sin as being serious nor found a place of true repentance, and because of that, he was on his way to hell. There was a quick way to find out—something I had done thousands of times. I would ask Duke if he thought he was a good person.

If you know anything about me, you know that I ask this question all the time. I'm doing it out of obedience. I'm not the only one aware that I have asked the same questions of sinners thousands of times. Someone who frequently watched our YouTube channel and saw me go through the routine of using the Ten Commandments wrote, "I've often been frustrated by Ray's approach because it is always the same." Think of *my* frustration. I have been saying the same thing to the lost since 1982. However, when I feel like a parrot, I remind myself that the person to whom I'm speaking hasn't heard this before. And I remind myself that this approach isn't mine; it's based on what Jesus did in Mark 10. He said to the rich young ruler in verse 19, "You know the commandments," and then He quoted five of the Ten Commandments. What I do is also based on the apostle Paul's questions in Romans 2:21–22: "You who preach that a [person] should not steal, do you steal? You who say, 'Do not commit adultery,' do you commit adultery?"

I ignored feeling like a parrot and asked Duke, "Are you a good person?" Sure enough, he said that he was a *very* good person, and that confirmed my concern. I took courage and asked how many lies he thought he had told. He said that he had told many. He had also stolen, used God's name in vain, and looked at women with lust. I then said, "Duke, I'm not judging you, but you've just told me that you are a lying, thieving, blasphemous adulterer at heart, and you have to face God on judgment day. If He judges you on that day by the Ten Commandments, are you going to be innocent or guilty?"

He said that he would be innocent "because I do good things."

I told him to try that in a court of law. "It's not going to help your case if you say to the judge that you're guilty of the serious crime of robbing a bank and shooting a guard, 'but I try to do good things for other people.'"

Then Duke said, "Well, there are plenty of people worse than me."

And I replied that if a police officer stopped him on the freeway for going eighty miles an hour, and he said to him in defense that there were plenty of drivers going faster, it would not hold water. And the same goes for God. He would be held *personally* responsible for his own crime. Everyone will have to give an account of *themselves*, not of other people, to God.

I then shared the gospel with him and told him that he was like a man planning to jump out of a plane and had a choice. Either he could flap his arms when he jumps to try to save himself, or he could trust in the parachute. I pleaded with dear adorable Duke to trust alone in Jesus and not try to save himself with his own goodness because he didn't have any in God's eyes.

He thanked me for talking to him and added, "I will think about this."

I gave him one of the books I had slipped into the glove box at the last minute and encouraged him to read it.

All this happened while I was sitting on the passenger side of our car, leaning toward the driver's side, and speaking through the window of the vehicle. It was kind of funny that I did that, but I was so glad I chose obedience over selfish fear.

THREE

Decisive

The Love Choice

But sanctify the Lord God in your hearts, and always be ready to give a defense to everyone who asks you a reason for the hope that is in you, with meekness and fear.

1 Peter 3:15

The Scriptures tell us to *always* be ready. We are to have a primed ear, a keen eye, a loving heart, a willing mind, and a ready tongue to give a reason for the hope that is within us. This isn't a defensive war. We are not to quietly wait for the world to *approach us* and ask for a reason as to why we believe what we believe. It's not normal to have fish come to you. You go to them. A man once told me that he was ready for when the lost approached him to ask about his faith in Jesus. I asked how many times that had happened in the previous twelve months. I wasn't surprised when he told me that no one had asked him about his faith. We are to *go* to them because we have been *commanded* to go (see Mark 16:15). We are to *advance*. Then we should be ready to answer questions.

First Peter 3:15 says to "always be ready." Scripture tells us when we are to reach out to the lost: *always*. First Corinthians 15:58 says, "My beloved brethren, be steadfast, immovable, *always abounding* in the work of the Lord, knowing that your labor is not in vain in the Lord" (emphasis added). Second Timothy 4:2 tells us to be ready *at all times*: "Preach the word! Be ready *in season and out of season*. Convince, rebuke, exhort, with all longsuffering and teaching" (emphasis added). First Peter 3:15 also gives us our field of endeavor: *everyone*. Don't write off a soul as hopeless.

Notice that the admonition doesn't say to give *the* reason. It says to give *a* reason. Here are a few of the many, many reasons I'm a Christian:

- *Without Jesus, I'm a dead man.* I'm dead in my trespasses and sins (see Eph. 2:1). Without God's amazing grace, His wrath remains on me, and I am justly destined for hell (see John 3:36).

- *Without a Savior, my understanding is darkened.* I'm alienated from the life of God through the ignorance that is in me because of the blindness of my heart (see Eph. 4:18). Without Jesus I'm blinded to the gospel, hopeless and helpless, held captive to sin and the devil, still in darkness—a child of disobedience (see 2 Cor. 4:4; 2 Tim. 2:26; Eph. 2:2).

- *With Jesus, I have everlasting life.* My sins are forgiven. I have joy unspeakable and peace that passes all understanding. I have a purpose in this life and a living hope in the next. I also have a *reason* to exist, praise the Lord. This brings me to tears of gratitude.

- *As a Christian, I'm no longer tormented by the fear of death*. It has no sting; the grave has no victory. I have a *living* hope. God has opened the eyes of my understanding, and He is now a reality. He is the lover of my soul, and I have the cross as evidence. The Scriptures are alive to me. The love of Jesus Christ not only dwells in my heart but also extends through me to the lost.

These are just a few drops in an ocean of reasons for the hope that is within me. What is your hope? Write down some of your reasons, so you will be ready.

Some Answers

If someone asks why you believe in God's existence, be ready with an answer. Be ready if you are asked why there is suffering, why Jesus is unique, why you need a Savior, or why Christianity is exclusive. The answers to each of these complex questions need not be an eloquent theological recitation. More often than not, they can be answered in a few sentences to the satisfaction of the questioner—if he or she really wants an answer. For example:

1. We believe in God's existence because it's scientifically impossible for nature to have made itself. Creation testifies to the genius of the Creator.

2. Suffering is stark evidence that the Bible is right when it says that we live in a fallen creation.

3. Jesus is unique because He claimed to be God, and He backed up this claim by displaying power over sickness, over nature, and over death. He also claimed preexistence.

4. In Christ, God provided a Savior in response to the law that we had violated. He paid the fine.

5. Christianity is exclusive because no other religion is based on grace—unmerited favor. *All* others are based on works. They teach that righteousness and eternal life can be earned—that the Judge of the universe can be bribed.

Maybe you think that Jesus would have given drawn-out answers. Keep in mind the example we have in Luke 13:1–5. When Jesus was asked a question about suffering, He didn't give a comprehensive answer. He simply told the questioners that they shouldn't come to their own conclusion about the issue. Instead, they should be more concerned about the suffering that was coming to them if they didn't repent. A man who is standing precariously on the edge of a plane ten thousand feet in the air shouldn't be asking questions. He should be putting on a parachute.

Choosing Love

Love is not only a fruit of the Spirit (see Gal. 5:22–23); it is also a choice. We *choose* to love the unsaved. We choose to always be ready to give an answer as to why we are trusting in Jesus Christ, and we do so in "meekness and fear." We have a trembling fear in our hearts because God Himself is trusting us with the gospel and because sinners will go to hell if they die in their sins. Evangelism should be mingled with both love and a healthy fear of God:

> And on some have *compassion*, making a distinction; *but others save with fear*, pulling them out of the fire, hating even the garment defiled by the flesh. (Jude 22–23, emphasis added)

> *Knowing, therefore, the terror of the Lord*, we persuade [others]; but we are well known to God, and I also trust are well known in your consciences. (2 Cor. 5:11, emphasis added)

But what makes our love so important? God didn't confine the virtue of love to human beings. Dogs love their owners, and they are not afraid to show it. A wagging tail can warm the coldest of human hearts. Birds, elephants, dolphins, and whales can exhibit even a *romantic* love. Male birds dance around prospective female beauties with amazing gestures and sounds that make human romance look shallow. Then there are lovebirds, who just sit together . . . like lovebirds. We don't have the corner on love, as National Geographic often reminds us with its photographic evidence: "Humans may have invented the most commercial love-themed holiday of all time, but we don't hold a monopoly on courtship. Many creatures go to great lengths or stage elaborate displays to woo an elusive mate."[1]

Jesus chose to go to the cross because of His great love for us. Love for God and for lost sinners overwhelmed His terrible fears in the garden of Gethsemane. And though the very thought of speaking to strangers about their salvation can almost cause us to sweat drops of blood, love chooses to overwhelm our fears as it whispers, "Not my will, but Yours be done." But let's pull back and bring these fears into proportion. Most of us are not going to be stoned to death for our faith. At worst, we may feel rejected if someone doesn't want to talk about the things of God. The massive mountain is a minuscule molehill, and we need to see it as such.

An article in *Time* magazine said of love:

It is time to change the meaning of the word "love."

The word is mostly used according to the first definition given in the dictionary: "an intense feeling of deep affection." In other words, love is what one feels.

After years spent speaking with couples before, during and after marriage; and of talking to parents and children struggling with their relationships, I am convinced of the partiality of the definition. Love should be seen not as a feeling but as an enacted emotion. To love is to feel and act lovingly.[2]

To love is also a choice we make. To love those we would normally not love, we must choose so decisively that our feelings actually change. Jesus told us to love our enemies (see Matt. 5:43–48). If we wait for a bubbly feeling to do that, we will be waiting for a long time. We must make a choice.

Many a marriage has found fire again after the initial spark fades. Dry sticks can produce flames if they are briskly rubbed together. In Ephesians 5, husbands are commanded to love their wives. The passage doesn't say to wait for the emotive *feeling* of love before doing so. This admonition is repeated three times: "Husbands, love your wives, just as

Christ also loved the church and gave Himself for her. . . . So husbands ought to love their own wives as their own bodies. . . . Let each one of you in particular so love his own wife as himself" (vv. 25, 28, 33). And in Titus 2:4, we read that older women are to tell younger women to love their husbands and children. In other words, we are to love by choice rather than wait for the feeling or emotion of love.

In choosing love, here is what we choose to usher into our lives: "Love suffers long and is kind; love does not envy; love does not parade itself, is not puffed up; does not behave rudely, does not seek its own, is not provoked, thinks no evil; does not rejoice in iniquity, but rejoices in the truth; bears all things, believes all things, hopes all things, endures all things" (1 Cor. 13:4–7). Choose these things—patience, kindness, humility of heart, courtesy, unselfishness, self-control, thankfulness, and truthfulness—and you will have a rich and loving marriage.

And the same applies to the lost. *Choose* to love them. Then, with the help of the Holy Spirit, exhibit these virtues. Exercise your decisive power. Be patient with the lost because they are blind, and remember that you yourself were once like them. Be kind to them because your kindness will speak louder than your words; it will enhance them. Have a humble attitude because almost everyone appreciates humility.

Barren Soil

Telling you this next story is, in a small way, a decision to be humble. I should have acted differently. In early November 2018, I rode my bike toward what looked like someone sitting on the bleachers at a baseball park. When I strained to see clearly, it didn't look right. But when I got close, I realized it was a shirtless man with his head almost between his knees. His skin was darkened with dirt. I felt uneasy and wondered if he might be unsafe.

As I got closer, I wanted to stop and talk to him, so I said, "Good morning." I knew I would find the courage to stop if he answered coherently. But there was no answer. He ignored me. I slowed down and asked if he was okay. Again, he treated me as though I didn't exist. I was conflicted. Wisdom told me not to approach him if I valued my life. I didn't want to end my time on earth by being stabbed by a madman.

But that is when I noticed the poor man's ribs. I could count each of them. I turned around, placed a Subway card at his feet, and said, "Here is some lunch for you."

As I rode away, I heard a gentle, "Thank you."

Since that day, his quiet "Thank you" has haunted me. How I wish I had stayed and tried to speak with him. Why was he so thin? Where was his family? How could I help him? Was he trusting in Jesus? But I chose the easy way out.

How far short most of us fall of the love exhibited by the "good" Samaritan, who stopped and helped the beaten man between Jericho and Jerusalem (see Luke 10:25–37). That poor man had been stripped and left for dead. But love stopped. It stayed. The Samaritan's gestures weren't just an appeasement of his conscience. Love poured oil and wine into his wounds. Love lifted him upon his own donkey, took him to an inn, and decided to pay for the broken man's expenses.

Compassion sees *every* unsaved human being as left for dead by the devil. It stops and pours in the oil and wine of the gospel. It denies itself and instead goes out of its way to speak to sinners. Love carries sinners to the safety of the cross. It doesn't move to the other side of the road out of selfishness or fear. It decides to kneel down next to anyone on the side of the road.

If we don't have love that weeps at the state and the fate of sinners, all of our giving, all of our theology, all of our professed worship isn't worth a hill of dry pharisaic beans:

> Though I speak with the tongues of men and of angels, but have not love, I have become sounding brass or a clanging cymbal. And though I have the gift of prophecy, and understand all mysteries and all knowledge, and though I have all faith, so that I could remove mountains, but have not love, I am nothing. And though I bestow all my goods to feed the poor, and though I give my body to be burned, but have not love, it profits me nothing. (1 Cor. 13:1–3)

May we all, especially me, be ever more ready and firmly decisive in our love toward all people.

The Mirror of the Law

Let's talk about another important decision we need to make. If I don't have a love that cries out for the unsaved, I would be wise to ask myself, *Am I truly saved?* Do I have the things that "accompany salvation" (see Heb. 6:9–12)? If I don't have the evident fruit, which is led by love, then I need to drop to my knees and plead with God that He show me my sin as it is.

When I suspect that someone is a false convert, I often ask this question: "Is your heart desperately wicked?" They will be quick to say that it isn't, that they are basically a good person. But we know better:

> The heart is deceitful above all things,
> And desperately wicked;
> Who can know it? (Jer. 17:9)

The problem with those who profess faith but lack fruit is that they've never seen sin as being *exceedingly* sinful (see Rom. 7:13). It was the moral law that showed the apostle Paul that he was exceedingly sinful, and it can do the same for each of us.

James speaks of those who profess faith but lack true repentance: "Therefore lay aside all filthiness and overflow of wickedness, and receive with meekness the implanted word, which is able to save your souls" (James 1:21).

He's addressing those who have never seen the filthiness of the pig food they desire. They have never acknowledged that their heart is overflowing with wickedness. James continues by pointing to the mirror of the law:

> Do not merely listen to the word, and so deceive yourselves. Do what it says. Anyone who listens to the word but does not do what it says is like someone who looks at his face in a mirror and, after looking at himself, goes away and immediately forgets what he looks like. But whoever looks intently into the perfect law that gives freedom, and continues in it—not forgetting what they have heard, but doing it—they will be blessed in what they do. (James 1:22–25 NIV)

Let's now look into the mirror of the law by listening to Jesus. Jesus opened up the law in the Sermon on the Mount. If you suspect that you have never been truly saved, let's walk up that mountain together, sit quietly at His feet, and listen to His amazing words as He expounds the demands of the moral law. For your convenience, I've included a passage from Matthew 5 here, the greatest sermon ever preached. Don't just read it; let it read you. Let it search your soul by asking yourself how far you fall short of its moral standard. Jesus is magnifying the law and making it honorable (see Isa. 42:21). He is enlarging the print so that we can see clearly its demands. As you read each verse, ask yourself the relevant questions: Do I see myself as being morally poverty-stricken? Do I mourn over my sins? Do I have an attitude of meekness—a willingness to humbly submit to God's will rather than my own? Do I hunger for righteousness and extend mercy to fellow human beings? Is my heart morally pure? Am I a peacemaker? Am I persecuted because I'm living a godly life in Christ Jesus? Am I the salt of the earth? Am I the light of the world? Am I letting my light shine?

Remember, these are evidences of godly character. If we are saved, these verses should bring us comfort because we possess these virtues in Christ. If we are not saved, they should bring a sense of conviction. An honest soul search will put us in the balance and leave us wanting. The finger of God will write on the walls of an accused conscience and have us fleeing to the mercy of the cross (see Gal. 3:24).

The Bible first sets the stage: "And seeing the multitudes, He went up on a mountain, and when He was seated His disciples came to Him. Then He opened His mouth and taught them, saying":

Blessed are the poor in spirit,
For theirs is the kingdom of heaven.

Blessed are those who mourn,
For they shall be comforted.

Blessed are the meek,
For they shall inherit the earth.

Blessed are those who hunger and thirst for righteousness,
For they shall be filled.

Blessed are the merciful,
For they shall obtain mercy.

Blessed are the pure in heart,
For they shall see God.

Blessed are the peacemakers,
For they shall be called sons of God.

Blessed are those who are persecuted for righteousness' sake,
For theirs is the kingdom of heaven.

Blessed are you when they revile and persecute you, and say
all kinds of evil against you falsely for My sake. Rejoice and
be exceedingly glad, for great is your reward in heaven, for
so they persecuted the prophets who were before you.

You are the salt of the earth; but if the salt loses its flavor,
how shall it be seasoned? It is then good for nothing but to
be thrown out and trampled underfoot by men.

You are the light of the world. A city that is set on a hill
cannot be hidden. Nor do they light a lamp and put it under
a basket, but on a lampstand, and it gives light to all who are
in the house. Let your light so shine before men, that they
may see your good works and glorify your Father in heaven.
(Matt. 5:1–14)

Now is the time for you to decide. Are you choosing to love the unsaved? Or do you need to look to the Savior for yourself?

The Blue Sky

It was a very pleasant Sunday afternoon in Southern California, with a little wind and an almost cloudless blue sky. As I rode my bike, I began formulating my springboard for a video interview. I often decide on an interesting and engaging question before I speak with people. I'd advise you to do the same. This particular day, I was feeling inspired by the good weather, and I decided I would talk about the blue sky: "Have you ever heard the saying "Familiarity breeds contempt"? That happens when something is so familiar to us that we take it for granted. We don't give it a second thought. One of these is a clear blue sky. We take it for granted. Have you ever looked at the sky and been overwhelmed by its beauty?" Then I would ask if the person ever thought about *who* made the sky: "Do you ever think about the greatness of God and what He requires of you?"

The first person I approached was sitting in an SUV smoking a cigarette. I rode up to him and said, "Would you be interested in doing an interview on YouTube?"

He said that he wouldn't. Not even for a free Subway card. Nor was he interested in giving his thoughts about the afterlife.

I said, "Okay. No camera. Do you think there's an afterlife?"

He said he didn't know.

I said, "Well, you're sure trying to hasten the day by smoking cigarettes."

He replied that he couldn't give up. He started when he was fourteen and he was now fifty years old. For the next few moments we talked about how teenagers feel grown up with a cigarette in their hand—how at that vulnerable age, a cigarette can give confidence and get you in with your buddies.

He then lifted up a bottle of beer to show me that he was also drinking as he sat in the car.

I said, "Are you sure you don't want to come on camera? You'd be a very interesting interview."

He was just as adamant about not doing an interview but said that he often came to the park just to sit in his car and have a smoke and drink alcohol, "and perhaps next time I see you we could have an interview."

I laughed and said that the next time he sees me he will probably hide.

He laughed at that, so I said, "Let me talk to you without the camera. If Heaven exists, are you going there? Are you a good person?"

He said that he was, but after we went through the Ten Commandments, he saw that he was guilty of lying, stealing, blasphemy, and committing adultery in his heart.

We then talked about his guilt on judgment day, how I cared about him, and how Christ died for sins. He said that he was a Roman Catholic, so I explained the difference between Catholicism and biblical Christianity. When I asked him if he had a Bible at home, he said he did but that it was small print and he didn't read much. I encouraged him to think about what we had talked about and gave him a Subway gift card for dinner that night.

After I left him, I kept my eyes peeled for someone to share my springboard about the blue sky. That's when I saw three young men standing at the top of the bleachers by the baseball field and did my usual approach about coming on camera. They were a little shy, but one seemed open. When I learned that all three were under eighteen and by law couldn't be filmed without parental consent, I said, "Sorry, you can't come on, even if you want to. You have to be over eighteen to be interviewed. But let me ask anyway. Do you think there's an afterlife?" Two of them did. But one (named Caleb) said he didn't think so. When I said that Caleb was a biblical name, he smiled and said that everyone keeps reminding him of that. He seemed confident and willing to listen, so I shared the gospel, making sure the others could hear. Even though they were about twenty feet from me, all three listened to a short gospel presentation.

"Caleb, how would you like a five-dollar Subway gift card for dinner tonight? I can give you each one."

They were clearly taken aback, came down from the bleachers, took the cards, then sat down in front of me as I shared the gospel in a little more detail—how Jesus paid the fine and God can now legally give us everlasting life.

"Any of you guys get suicidal thoughts?"

Caleb said that he did, so I left him my book on how to battle depression and suicidal thoughts.

I didn't get to share my clear-blue-sky springboard, but I did get to share the clear gospel, and for that I was grateful.

Three weeks later, Sam and I set out on the bike, and I prayed that God would direct me to someone. I rode past a car with the driver's side window down, and I heard someone cussing very loudly. I turned around and approached the vehicle. It was my smoking, beer-drinking friend. He looked at me and said, "You caught me!"

I smiled and asked what the problem was. It turned out that a bee had gotten into his car.

He said, "I was scared that it was going to sting me, and I'm allergic to bees!" He gave me some background, explaining that when he was a kid he was stung on the forehead and his whole face swelled up.

I said, "You know who's in charge of bees, don't you?" I pointed to the heavens and added, "Maybe God sent him to you as a wake-up call."

He agreed. I asked if he had read the book I had given him two weeks earlier, and he said he didn't like reading. He got the book out of his glove box and showed it to me.

"That bee could have killed you. It should have put the fear of God in you, because that's what you need. I have a friend who had an aneurysm when he was sixteen. He was at school and fell to the ground. The doctors thought he had banged his head, but it was an aneurysm, and for the last twelve years he's been paralyzed from the neck down. He's unable to talk or even eat. That could happen to any of us—this is *serious* business. So think about the fact that you could die at any time and your need to seriously consider your salvation." This man needed to be decisive. But we never would have had that conversation if I hadn't been decisive in my evangelism, always ready to share my faith.

FOUR

Defiant

Fighting the Real Enemy

Put on the whole armor of God, that you may be able to stand against the wiles of the devil.

Ephesians 6:11

It was very strange. In the space of four days, I interviewed three people who either had been shot or had shot other people. The first was a man named Jeff. He was in his late fifties, and he'd been confined to a wheelchair for the last twenty years because he'd been shot four times. He was sitting at a light in his car at 5:00 a.m. when someone decided they would steal it. He was shot, dragged from the vehicle, and left for dead on the side of the road. He had tattooed bullet holes over the four points of bullet entry into the side of his body, and he was very open to the gospel and very friendly.

The second man, Shaun, was sitting with a woman in the bleachers at the local baseball park. Shaun wasn't so friendly. *Volatile* would be more applicable. He had just been released from prison after serving time for killing someone. Apparently, he got into a fight and punched him, and the man died. During our interview, he boasted of shooting five people at a convenience store back in 1993. I suspected that this man was brimming with demons. At one point, he said there was a time in his life when he could have taken me out so quickly, I wouldn't have known what hit me. Needless to say, I spoke to him very gently.

The third incident began well. "Smirk" was very friendly, had a great smile, and talked about how we should all love each other. He had been shot five times with a 9mm handgun, and he said that when it happened, he hadn't prayed, cried, or fallen down. But during the interview, I made a big mistake. After we went through the Commandments, he showed me his scars, and I asked, "Was it from a robbery?" He suddenly became angry, cussed, and started telling his friend behind me about how I had crossed the line. Apparently, mentioning robbery was the limit. He had been released from prison a day earlier and was fuming beyond the point of being reasoned with. I stopped the interview and felt fortunate that I wasn't beaten and left for dead. I'll tell you the rest of that story at the end of the chapter. My encounter with Smirk gave me plenty of opportunities to be defiant against the real enemy.

When the world describes men like Shaun or Smirk, they will often use the phrase "he has his demons" metaphorically. Christians use it literally.

Look at how the *Amplified Bible* amplifies Ephesians 6:11: "Put on the full armor of God [for His precepts are like the splendid armor of a heavily-armed soldier], so that you may be able to [successfully] stand up against all the schemes and the strategies and the deceits of the devil."

God's Word gives us insight into the schemes, strategies, and deceits of the devil. Without it, we would be spiritually ignorant. We wouldn't know how to go into battle. We couldn't be defiant.

Isolationism

During the 1930s after WWI and the Depression, American public opinion and policy tended toward isolationism. Isolationists pushed for noninvolvement in world conflicts and nonentanglement in international politics.

The Nazis didn't want the United States to enter the second terrible war that was brewing in Europe, so they infiltrated the country and stoked the fires of isolationism. President Roosevelt spoke of these infiltrators:

> They came in different sizes and shapes, he explained. One group of them constituted a Trojan horse of pro-German spies, saboteurs, and traitors. While not naming names, he singled out those who sought to arouse people's "hatred" and "prejudices" by resorting to "false slogans and emotional appeals." With fifth columnists who sought to "divide and weaken us in the face of danger," Roosevelt declared, "we must and will deal vigorously." Another group of isolationists, he explained, opposed his administration's policies

simply for the sake of opposition—even when the security of the nation stood at risk.[1]

Isolationism is alive and well in the contemporary church. False converts sit in pews and stand in pulpits. You will encounter the demonic influence controlling these false converts if you begin to talk about entering the war. I have lost count of the soldiers of Christ who have been forced to leave their churches because they were discouraged from reaching out to those who have been taken prisoner by the enemy (2 Tim. 2:26). Sadly, these churches want to remain isolated from the world we have been told to reach.

Discouragement has a spiritual source. If we lose sight of that, we will fall into the trap of battling other people when *they* aren't the enemy. I often have to avoid that trap. I run into people who think I'm the enemy too. I remember speaking for about forty minutes to someone who stood on our heckler's box at Huntington Beach. (We have two soapboxes—one for the preacher and one for the heckler). It had been an interesting dialogue. As I sat down for a break, a man who professed faith in Jesus struck up a conversation with me. What he said was predictable. He was an isolationist who thought that preaching to sinners was unbiblical. He said we shouldn't confront the world but simply pray for them instead.

But praying for sinners and never sharing the gospel is like having the cure to cancer and never giving it to the patient. Scripture asks, "How shall they hear without a preacher?" (Rom. 10:14). What does the silent believer, like that man on Huntington Beach, pray for? Does he pray that sinners would hear the gospel and be saved? Even if these silent believers aren't our enemies, they are often *tools* of the enemy, sent to discourage those who fight the good fight of faith. Guarding our hearts against their discouragement is part of wearing the whole armor of God and being able to stand against the wiles of the devil.

The Way of the Transgressor

The Bible says that the way of the transgressor is hard. They bring on themselves unnecessary pain and suffering—from taking in the toxins of alcohol, tobacco, and other poisons to human conflicts that could be avoided if the virtue of love was present. Demons of hatred, lust, greed, bitterness, envy, and jealousy have free access into their minds and out of their mouths. Because they don't believe what Scripture says about sin and the enemy they battle, they fall en masse into the graves of destroyed marriages and broken friendships. Every day, headlines around the world announce those who are victims of the one who came to kill, steal, and destroy.

Jesus spoke of the ungodly as walking in darkness, stumbling without knowing what they stumbled over. He said, "Are there not twelve hours in the day? If anyone walks in the day, he does not stumble, because he sees the light of this world. But if one walks in the night, he stumbles, because the light is not in him" (John 11:9–10).

Their choice to stay in darkness disqualifies them from so many things that we in the light take for granted. We have a heart of contentment and thanksgiving, not just because we have been told to be content and thankful but because we have the cross as evidence of God's love. That fortifies us against the wiles of greed and selfish ambition.

We have love in our marriages and in our relationships with those around us. That means we extend grace and have mercy toward others, which guard us against the wiles of self-destructive bitterness, jealousy, and hatred.

We respect the temple that God gave us and stay away from the demons of alcohol and mind-destroying drugs. Our ideal isn't hedonism and the smile of the world but righteousness and the smile of God. We guard our hearts with all diligence by keeping them free from the seeds of lust and selfishness that grow into trees with poisonous fruit.

We also know that life has purpose. We were created by God to enjoy eternity. This knowledge causes us to *value* this life. "The ungodly are not so, but are like the chaff which the wind drives away" (Ps. 1:4). They are ignorantly blown about by demonic influences and don't value life as a gift from God. Past generations believed we were made in the image of God, but the enemy has convinced many in today's world that they are merely evolving beasts, the random result of an explosion of nothing caused by nothing. Therefore, life becomes futile, and with no fear of God before their eyes, they are nothing but time bombs of hopelessness. We, on the other hand, know the truth. The truth makes us defiant toward the enemy and those who are under his control.

One suicidal young lady told me that her aunt had taken her own life. According to the note she left, one of the reasons this woman had committed suicide was that she was tired of cleaning her teeth. That sounds strange, but it is understandable for anyone whose foundation is not God. If there is no ultimate purpose, no hope in death, then life becomes a drudge and death is an escape from a downward spiral of futility. That is the tragic fruit of the thankless, selfish, godless existence of someone who refuses to believe the testimony of the Bible.

A Good Snooze

I *despise* the necessity of having to sleep. Every sixteen hours of our precious lives, we are forced to yield eight hours to an unconscious state that takes us into a world of insanity.

If you're a control freak, or even if you *like* being in control, you should dislike sleep because you give up control of your mind—your decision center. Something else has the remote control and changes the channel. You don't know what entertainment you will have that night. It may be a night of horror, leaving you dripping with sweat and your heart beating out of your chest. It may be R-rated, causing you to transgress your tender conscience. It may be an unsolved mystery, leaving you wondering what it was all about.

And when you do wake up, you feel and look worse than when you went to sleep. If you don't believe that, look into a mirror first thing in the morning.

Jesus likened death to sleep (see John 11:11). While that's comforting, because the analogy tells us that death isn't permanent for the believer, it is also somewhat applicable. When we are asleep, we may as well be dead because we accomplish nothing—unless we get a fat-cows-swallowing-thin-cows dream that is divinely inspired (along with an interpretation; see Gen. 41). But those are few and far between.

Because of this contempt for sleep, I have (since 1982) gotten up for a while most nights to pray. Afterward, I write books or edit videos. If I'm ever tempted to think I'm a spiritual giant because I do this, I'm reminded that *millions* get up each night because they work a graveyard shift. This is one of my ways of turning darkness into light. Each morning, I wake up knowing that I have overcome futility and accomplished something in the night.

We know that the enemy came to *steal* (see John 10:10), and so we want to defend time because it is our most valuable commodity. We need to be defiant about our time, so we can use it for God's purposes. We value it because we will soon be in eternity. We are to *redeem* the time (see Eph. 5:16). The word *redeem* means to "compensate for the faults or bad aspects of" something.[2]

The *Amplified Bible* puts the verse this way: "Making the very most of your time [on earth, recognizing and taking advantage of each opportunity and using it with wisdom and diligence], because the days are [filled with] evil."

John Wesley (1703–91) is one of my heroes. He loved God, and he loved sinners enough to plead with them in the open air whenever he could. He redeemed the time. Look at his tirade against sleep:

> "See that ye walk circumspectly," says the Apostle in the preceding verse, "not as fools, but as wise men, redeeming

the time"; saving all the time you can for the best purposes; buying up every fleeting moment out of the hands of sin and Satan, out of the hands of sloth, ease, pleasure, worldly business; the more diligently, because the present "are evil days," days of the grossest ignorance, immorality, and profaneness.

This seems to be the general meaning of the words. But I purpose, at present, to consider only one particular way of "redeeming the time," namely, from sleep.

This appears to have been exceeding little considered, even by pious men. Many that have been eminently conscientious in other respects, have not been so in this. They seemed to think it an indifferent thing, whether they slept more or less; and never saw it in the true point of view, as an important branch of Christian temperance.[3]

Wesley quotes William Law (1686–1761), another one of my historical faith heroes:

Sleep is such a dull, stupid state of existence, that, even among mere animals, we despise them most which are most drowsy. He, therefore, that chooses to enlarge the slothful indolence of sleep, rather than be early at his devotions, chooses the dullest refreshment of the body, before the noblest enjoyments of the soul. He chooses that state which is a reproach to mere animals, before that exercise which is the glory of angels.[4]

I share these thoughts about sleep to give you a practical way to be defiant. Are you sleeping more than your health requires? Get up, pray, and listen for what God wants you to do with all the extra time you can give Him.

The Cause of Isolationism

One great weapon that will help us to be defiant against the enemy and to resist isolationism is to remember our past sins, lest we forget how to empathize with the lost. Though a new creature in Christ, the apostle Paul never forgot why he needed the Savior: "Christ Jesus came into the world to save sinners, of whom I am chief" (1 Tim. 1:15).

While it's true that our sins are forgiven and forgotten by God, the apostle didn't say "of whom I *was* chief." He used the word *am.*

I love the way Scripture tells us that our salvation comes by the grace of God. Paul presents grace like a glorious sunrise. He begins his buildup to the famous verses of Ephesians 2:8–9 with "And you He made alive, who were dead in trespasses and sins" (v. 1).

We were once dead in our trespasses and sins. We *earned* our wages. But Jesus called us out of the grave to follow Him. Scripture tells us that before He raised four-days-dead Lazarus from the grave, Jesus *groaned:* "Therefore, when Jesus saw her weeping, and the Jews who came with her weeping, *He groaned in the spirit* and was troubled. . . . Then Jesus, *again groaning in Himself,* came to the tomb" (John 11:33, 38, emphasis added).

Do we have that virtue? Do we *groan* from the weight of empathy? Sinners are dead in their sins, like an army of dry bones. If we want them to hear the Word of the Lord from our lips, our words must be impassioned. We should groan over the past and the future of lost sinners. Where *we* were in the past will direct how we handle the present. We *remember* where we once were: we "once walked according to the course of this world, according to the prince of the power of the air, the spirit who now works in the [children] of disobedience, among whom also we all once conducted ourselves in the lusts of our flesh, fulfilling the desires of the flesh and of the mind, and were by nature children of wrath, just as the others" (Eph. 2:2–3).

I shudder as I think of my BC (Before Christ) days. I shudder because of the testimony of Holy Scripture. I once lived for nothing but the selfish lusts of my flesh, "fulfilling the desires of the flesh and of the mind." As with others in the secular world, I thought life was all about me and my friends and our pleasures. Nothing else really mattered. As teenagers, we partied. We looked for girls, and girls looked for us. We drank alcohol at night and boasted the next day of sinful achievements. We walked according to the ways of this world, willingly doing the will of the god of this world, and in doing so unwittingly storing up the just wrath of God: "But in accordance with your hardness and your impenitent heart you are treasuring up for yourself wrath in the day of wrath and revelation of the righteous judgment of God, who 'will render to each one according to his deeds'" (Rom. 2:5–6).

I tremble to think that if I had died in my sins, I would have been justly damned. Because of my past, I cannot condemn this present world. Nor can any other Christian. We can't look down our sanctified noses for a second. We can't judge their weird hair and silly clothes, their filthy language and mockery, their greed and lust, or their hatred of the light and natural love of pleasure. On the contrary, we *empathize* with their blindness because we were once blind too. *But for the grace of God*, there go I. Grace reached out and saved me while I was yet a sinner. My spirituality and sanctification since the hour I first believed did nothing to earn my salvation. God's amazing grace silences our bragging. Instead, we whisper, "Not of works, lest anyone should boast" (Eph. 2 9).

Memories of my sinful life turn me away from isolationism. I walk in the light, but my sinful past is a dark shadow that follows me and reminds me of mercy: "But God, who is rich in mercy, because of His great love with which He loved us, even when we were dead in trespasses, made us alive together with Christ (by grace you have been saved), and raised us up together, and made us sit together in the heavenly places in Christ Jesus" (vv. 4–6). The full glorious sun then rises over the horizon as Paul speaks about the splendor of grace: "That in the ages to come He might show the exceeding riches of His grace in His kindness toward us in Christ Jesus. For by grace you have been saved through faith, and that not of yourselves; it is the gift of God, not of works, lest anyone should boast. For we are His workmanship, created in Christ Jesus for good works, which God prepared beforehand that we should walk in them" (vv. 7–10).

We weren't saved *by* good works but *for* good works. We weren't saved because we repented or because we believed. We were saved by grace alone. It was unearned, undeserved, and unwarranted, and it came to us while we were unthankful, ungrateful, and unholy. God pitied us. He loved us, not because we were lovable but because *He* is love. He loved us while we joyfully served sin. He loved us while we were wicked.

He loved us just as He presently loves this wicked world. That's why we must never forget our past; we must be defiant in our memories:

> *Therefore remember* that you, once Gentiles in the flesh— who are called Uncircumcision by what is called the Circumcision made in the flesh by hands—that at that time you were without Christ, being aliens from the commonwealth of Israel and strangers from the covenants of promise, having no hope and without God in the world. But now in Christ Jesus you who once were far off have been brought near by the blood of Christ. (vv. 11–13, emphasis added)

Think of Their Fate

Most of us—well, those of us who are awake!—like to be in control. We like to be in control of our car, the TV remote control, our finances, and our health. But as life unfolds, we realize there are certain things that are out of our control— like our own deaths.

For the sinner, the fear of death casts a long and dark shadow. As time passes, they come to realize that every pleasure they strive for is temporary and unsustainable. It is, as Solomon said, like chasing the wind.

The ungodly will follow this hopelessness all the way to hell. This fact should break our hearts and drive us to defiant action. But we are so entangled in our own desires that we don't make the time to think about the fate of the lost, let alone seek them out and plead with them. We forget our own past, dismissing the lost as sinners who deserve hell.

Just before I came to faith in Jesus, I was strongly drawn into Indian culture because of the influence of The Beatles. I was desperately seeking truth, and in retrospect I realize I was being influenced by seducing spirits. The unsaved are not the enemy—these evil spirits are. I was once in darkness, alienated from the life of God through the ignorance that was in me because of the blindness of my heart. But someone had the kindness to think of my fate. Are you thinking of the fate of others? Or are you condemning sinners who are being led astray by the real enemy?

A merciful and compassionate attitude produces a groaning prayer life and motivates us to reach out with the gospel. An effective evangelist doesn't condemn sinners; an effective evangelist defies the enemy!

I want to end the chapter by telling you the rest of the Smirk story. God gave me the confidence to be defiant, and I want you to see what that looks like in practice.

Remember my serious mistake with Smirk? When we went through the Ten Commandments, he admitted to stealing. I had asked if his scars were the result of a robbery, and that's when I crossed a gangster line. Such a personal question angered him.

The brunt of his anger came out a few minutes later. His facial expression changed. He was no longer smiling. He looked at his friend, who was standing behind me, and said cynically with his teeth together, "Hey . . . look at this guy over here. See this guy? He won't stop recording me. I told him I don't want to talk no more, and he keeps recording me." I quickly put the camera down and turned it off. I gave him two Subway cards instead of one as a small apology for my offense, hoping to at least get his smile back, but it didn't happen. He merely took the cards and, in anger, stormed off. I was disappointed that he hadn't stayed to hear the gospel and that I didn't have a positive conclusion to an otherwise interesting interview.

I combined another interview with his, and we released a short teaser on our YouTube channel, something we often do.

About three weeks later, I was in the same area of the local park and managed to capture a wonderful interview with two girls. Both of them had been raised in Christian homes but had strayed. After about ten minutes, one of them said that her parents were Christians and that they would be delighted with our talk. As we parted, I called out, "May I film you walking away? It will make a nice conclusion to your interview."

As I was filming them walking away, Smirk suddenly appeared in my peripheral, and he was so angry it made our first meeting seem like a tea party. He had seen the trailer and stated that I had told him I wouldn't post his interview online. What I had actually said to him that day was that I would turn the camera off, which I did. Unfortunately for me, he misunderstood what I said. If he had asked me to delete what we'd filmed that day, I would have done so on the spot right in front of him so that I wouldn't be tempted to use it.

The camera had been rolling during his tirade. Because I was threatened, I sent the original interview and the new footage to my advisory board for safekeeping. Here is the word-for-word transcript of our second encounter (my words are in italics):

Hey, how are you doing?

Why are you posting the video of me?

You shouldn't be on. [We had posted only the trailer.]

You told me you weren't going to post that video of me.

Oh, I'm very sorry.

Why did you post that %#*!#?

Huh? I'm very sorry.

You told me that you weren't going to post that %#*!#!

I don't think I did.

You better %#*!# delete my %#*!#. If I catch you here
again, I'll %#*!# your %#*!#. You hear me? %#*!#

Yes sir.

The %#*!# my %#*!# face!

Thank you.

You need to keep your %#*!# word to people, homie.
Lying %#*!# %#*!#!

Then he stormed off, yelling about my indiscretions to whoever could hear him in the distance.

During this encounter, the two girls I had interviewed courageously stepped between him and me. I was both humbled
and grateful because if they hadn't done that, I'm sure I
would have had my face rearranged. I had used my best "a
soft answer turns away wrath" (Prov. 15:1), but I was aware
during the incident that I would have been easy pickings
because I was holding the bike and steadying Sam, who was
sitting on the platform on the bike. I wouldn't have been able
to block any blows to my face.

After seeing the footage, my manager wrote back, "That
was crazy!!!! Maybe you should take a break from going to

that location for a while? 'A prudent man foresees the evil, and hides himself: but the simple pass on and are punished' (Prov. 22:3).''

I had already told Sue that I would stay away from there for a while. I thought about how I had stumbled upon too many drug deals and interviewed too many doped-up people and how three different people in a matter of a few days had shown me multiple bullet wounds. I'd also noticed a couple of regulars getting a little impatient with me.

What happened was quite scary, so it was a relief to make a decision to go to a different part of town. At the same time, I felt sad. I had filmed some amazing interviews in the park with all kinds of people. Many times I would come back from filming carefully holding my phone, knowing that I had just recorded precious footage that potentially could bring many to the Savior. At that time, our YouTube channel had just passed sixty-five million views, and it was exploding. Every day, Christians left comments saying they were being equipped and emboldened to share their faith, and now and then unsaved people would leave comments saying that the clips were bringing them to God. The park was truly a godsend for me. And here was a demonically possessed man threatening physical harm if I showed up there again. I kept thinking about his threat: "If I catch you here again I'll %#*!# your %#*!#. You hear me? %#*!#"

Why would he say that? It didn't make sense—unless my wrestle wasn't against flesh and blood. I decided that Goliath wasn't going to intimidate me. I kept my word to Sue and my manager by taking a break from the park. But it was only for a day.

I took courage and went back the next day, and the first person I asked to come on camera was more than willing to be interviewed. He was a very open and polite engineering student from Berkeley University whose name was Nathan. The name means "gift from God," and I certainly felt that the park was a God-given gift. Besides, I had always admired the courage of Nathan the prophet in the Bible. He did what he knew he should do, trusted the Lord, and let the chips fall where they may. Twice during the interview, I had fearful thoughts of Smirk showing up while I was speaking, but I ignored them. I was going to be defiant. Against the real enemy, I would stand my ground.

FIVE

Focused

Eyes on the Cross

For we do not wrestle against flesh and blood, but against principalities, against powers, against the rulers of the darkness of this age, against spiritual hosts of wickedness in the heavenly places.

Ephesians 6:12

A survey by Barna Research late in 2018 found that things weren't too rosy with the spiritual state of the youth: "Teenagers today are the most non-Christian generation in American history as only four out of 100 teens hold a true biblical worldview and one out of every eight teens identify as non-heterosexual."[1] Barna's research discovered that more teens today, part of Generation Z (born from 1999 to 2015), identify themselves as agnostic, atheist, or not religiously affiliated.

These statistics shouldn't come as a shock. Most of today's youth are ignorant of the biblical gospel because most of today's churches haven't taken the gospel to them. The unsaved are in darkness because we have kept the light to ourselves. The report continues: "Teens are beginning to feel like they have to choose between science and the Bible, where as the Baby Boomer generation or Gen X said that they can see the Bible and science as being complementary. . . . When we get to millennials and Gen Z, they see them in conflict."[2]

The conflict isn't between science and the Bible. It's between unscientific, unproven, and unprovable Darwinian evolution and the Bible. When the average unbeliever speaks of a clash between evolution and Scripture, he's not thinking about science—speciation and adaptation. The Bible doesn't disagree with these scientific processes.

Speciation is differences within a kind. For example, the dog kind is made up of many different types of dogs—from the tiny Chihuahua to the Great Dane. That's not Darwinian evolution, and there is no clash with the Bible. Speciation is everywhere.

Neither is there a conflict in regard to adaptation. Birds have beaks that *adapt* to their surroundings. Many animals also adapt to their surroundings. There is no clash with the Bible or with Christianity. We see adaptation everywhere.

The clash is with Darwin's proposal that human beings and primates have a common ancestor (that humans are primates). There isn't *any* empirical evidence for that theory, not even a bone of contention. The entire theory rests on blind faith—not on science. It doesn't pass the standard scientific method. It cannot be observed or tested. How can anyone test or observe something that supposedly happened millions of years ago?

What the Bible claims, however, does pass the scientific method. It says that God created male and female. We can observe and test that in the existing creation. Scripture also says that every animal brings forth after its own kind. We can observe and test that in the existing creation. Nothing is changing kind. Dogs always reproduce dogs. Cats always reproduce cats. It's the same with horses, cows, lions, monkeys, and so on. Nothing changes kinds, just as the Scriptures say.

Yet, this sinful generation sees the Bible and science as incompatible. The god of this world convinced them that the theory of evolution is true when it is a fantasy, and that the Bible is fantasy when it's true.

One of the conclusions of the Barna study is that many of today's youth are embracing the foolishness of atheism. And one of the biggest lies of the enemy is that atheism is somehow intellectual.

We have a deceived and brainwashed generation that has given itself to seducing spirits and is blinded to the truth, hating God without cause. But as we said in the last chapter, we are not fighting *against* them. We are fighting *for* them. They are not the enemy. We wrestle not against the flesh and blood of this generation but against evil that has possessed humanity for generations. The same snakes that hissed at Stephen, that hissed through Saul of Tarsus, hiss at us. Here's the real challenge for Christians today: we are in a war, but most of the army doesn't believe in the cause.

In my practice of evangelism, I sympathize with those who have the difficult task of advertising high-definition television on TV. The only way the viewer will see the quality of the picture is if he is watching it on a high-definition screen, and if he already has a high-definition screen, he's not a potential customer. And if he's watching the advertisement on a low-definition screen, he is not going to see the quality of the picture. It's a lose-lose situation.

We have a similar problem when we evangelize. We are taking the highest-quality message to those who are spiritually blind and don't want to see it. But our confidence isn't in our eloquence; it's in the power of the gospel and the faithfulness of God. Therefore, we never lose heart, even for a minute—*because God is with us*. And if God is with us, nothing can be against us (see Rom. 8:31). He sought us out, found us, and extended the mercy of the cross. If He did that for us, He will do it for other sinners:

> Therefore, since we have this ministry, as we have received mercy, we do not lose heart. But we have renounced the hidden things of shame, not walking in craftiness nor handling the word of God deceitfully, but by manifestation of the truth commending ourselves to every man's conscience in the sight of God. But even if our gospel is veiled, it is veiled to those who are perishing, whose minds the god of this age has blinded, who do not believe, lest the light of the gospel of the glory of Christ, who is the image of God, should shine on them. (2 Cor. 4:1–4)

The unsaved are unsaved because the god of this world has blinded their minds to the gospel. That's why they are in darkness. When presented in truth, the gospel is a light that shines on them. We want them to understand what is at stake.

A good evangelist maintains focus. It's important for us to understand the ins and outs of the evolution debate, but if you get into a conversation with the lost about evolution, don't stay there. Get to the gospel. It's the power of God unto salvation (see Rom. 1:16). It is there that they will see the light and the love of God in Christ. It's encouraging when other Christians grasp this essential truth. I found the following short discourse in the comments section of our YouTube channel:

> Steven C.: Ray missed the clue this man was giving when he told Ray, "I'm trying to get my life on track right now." Ray should have dug deeper with relevant questions about why his life is off track and taken it from there. But I know he has to keep these short and concise and to the point of the gospel.

> Susan C.: If Ray were a buddy of his only, or if Ray were acting as a pastor, yes, that would be a good place to go. But I like to stick with the law and the gospel. Know why? I've watched so many of these, I did a practice run with a Christian friend and did really well! But when I get too sidetracked, such as with someone I see about twice a week for several hours, I end up losing focus. And what is our focus to be? The Good News. You can always have more in-depth talks once people are saved and then have questions. It's a lot harder to get that message across if you delve into things a therapist would ask, such as "Oh? Why is your life off track?" or "In what way is your life off track?" Evangelism and biblical counseling are really quite different. Biblical counseling takes a lot of learning too.

One hindrance to evangelism is that we have made apologetics the issue rather than the simplicity of the gospel. We lack focus. Many potential laborers remain in the pews because they don't believe they have the intellectual capacity to argue about atheism and evolution. But Jesus didn't say to go into all the world and *intellectually convince* the world that the Bible is the Word of God or that evolution isn't true. He said to preach the *gospel* to every creature (see Mark 16:15).

The war we fight isn't intellectual; it is moral. It's not carnal, but spiritual, and therefore it has a spiritual solution. To continually address the subject of evolution is to attack the branches and ignore the root. "For we do *not* wrestle against flesh and blood," so don't *fight* flesh and blood: "For though we walk in the flesh, we do not war according to the flesh. For the weapons of our warfare are not carnal but mighty in God for pulling down strongholds" (2 Cor. 10:3–4).

Think of the battle of the early church. Stephen had been stoned to death. When Saul of Tarsus witnessed his death, it stirred his demons: "Then Saul, still breathing threats and murder against the disciples of the Lord, went to the high priest and asked letters from him to the synagogues of Damascus, so that if he found any who were of the Way, whether men or women, he might bring them bound to Jerusalem" (Acts 9:1–2).

Put yourself in the position of the first-century church. Saul was a bloodthirsty murderer who would stop at nothing to remove them from the face of the earth. It would have been easy to see only Saul. But they knew that the battle wasn't against this homicidal maniac. He was merely the tool of the demonic world, and he needed to hear the gospel. He had to be confronted with its life-changing power, and that is what happened on the road to Damascus:

As he journeyed he came near Damascus, and suddenly a light shone around him from heaven. Then he fell to the ground, and heard a voice saying to him, "Saul, Saul, why are you persecuting Me?"

And he said, "Who are You, Lord?"

Then the Lord said, "I am Jesus, whom you are persecuting. It is hard for you to kick against the goads."

So he, trembling and astonished, said, "Lord, what do You want me to do?"

Then the Lord said to him, "Arise and go into the city, and you will be told what you must do."

And the men who journeyed with him stood speechless, hearing a voice but seeing no one. Then Saul arose from the ground, and when his eyes were opened he saw no one. But they led him by the hand and brought him into Damascus. And he was three days without sight, and neither ate nor drank. (vv. 3–9)

When we present the gospel to a sinner and they come to faith in Christ, we are giving them their own Damascus road experience. They, like Saul of Tarsus, are on the road to damnation—in their own state of enmity against God (see Rom. 8:7). But when the gospel shines on them, it blinds them to everything but Jesus. We take them by the hand and lead them because they are blind.

Paul didn't simply come to Jesus without the soil of his heart first being turned by the moral law. He said he didn't have any idea as to the nature of sin without the law (see Rom. 3:19–20; 7:7), and that by it, sin became "exceedingly sinful" and brought him to a point of death (Rom. 7:13). The law cast a great shadow of death over him and prepared his heart for the light of the glorious gospel of Christ, who is the image of God. It was a schoolmaster to bring him to Christ (see Gal. 3:24).

Preach Christ Crucified

The famous actor Morgan Freeman needs no introduction. His deep, rich voice is ideal for heady topics like religion. The National Geographic Channel had picked a winner for their program, *The Story of God*. He carries a certain authority: "Academy Award winner Morgan Freeman explores the meaning of life, God, and many big questions in between in an effort to understand how religion has evolved and shaped society. A different divine subject is covered in each hourlong episode, titles of which include 'Creation,' 'The Devil Inside,' 'Afterlife,' 'Apocalypse,' and 'Who Is God?'"[3]

It was for that reason I cynically passed up *The Story of God* on the menu for months. I refused to even look at the program, and not just because it was the world. It was the National Geographic, and on top of that, it was Hollywood.

But one day I clicked on it. I watched only one episode in the series, "Apocalypse,"[4] and was pleasantly surprised. There was no blasphemy, no interviewing of atheists, and no talk of evolution. It was just a respectful look at different religions, with Buddhism getting a thumbs-up. Buddhism was presented as a peacefully passive religion that doesn't talk about morality, sin, judgment day, or hell. Mr. Freeman even interviewed a young man who sat crossed-legged and hummed for most of his time on the program. He was addressed as "holiness," but when it came to talking about truth, this poor man was nothing but a lost and bewildered sinner. This was interpreted by Mr. Freeman as humility.

They spoke together for sixty minutes, seeking truth, looking at religions, discussing various opinions and enlightened experts, and humming, and they didn't once mention Jesus or what He said. The only reference in the entire program was from a Jew who pointed across Jerusalem to the place where Jesus resorted with His disciples. To produce a program on religions of the world and leave out Jesus is like doing a program on oceans and leaving out water.

The hordes of hell don't care how holy you are, how much you hum, or how deeply you dive into apologetics, as long as you stay away from preaching Christ crucified. That's the light they don't want you to shine, *because that is the core of the gospel, which is the power of God unto salvation.*

Exalt the Savior

First Timothy 3:16 tells us who Jesus is: "And without controversy great is the mystery of godliness: *God was manifest in the flesh*, justified in the Spirit, seen by angels, preached among the Gentiles, believed on in the world, received up in glory" (KJV, emphasis added). But if you ask the world who Jesus is, you will get a slew of answers—a complete fiction, a historical figure, a deceiver, a great teacher, the Son of God, a prophet, the brother of Lucifer, the Son of Man, and more. Rarely will you hear Him referred to as the Creator of the universe. But that is who Scripture says He is: "He is the image of the invisible God, the firstborn over all creation. *For by Him all things were created that are in heaven and that are on earth*, visible and invisible, whether thrones or dominions or principalities or powers. All things were created through Him and for Him" (Col. 1:15–16, emphasis added). And in Hebrews 1, we read:

> God, who at various times and in various ways spoke in time past to the fathers by the prophets, has in these last days spoken to us by His Son, whom He has appointed heir of all things, *through whom also He made the worlds*; who being the brightness of His glory and the express image of His person, and upholding all things by the word of His power, when He had by Himself purged our sins, sat down at the right hand of the Majesty on high. (vv. 1–3, emphasis added)

Here is Hebrews 1:2 in the *Amplified Bible*: "Through whom also He created the universe [that is, the universe as a space-time-matter continuum]."

The entire universe—including the trillions upon trillions of stars and planets in the infinitude of space—was created by Jesus Christ.

> In the beginning was the Word, and the Word was with God, and the Word was God. The same was in the beginning with God. *All things were made by him; and without him was not any thing made that was made.* . . . And the Word was made flesh, and dwelt among us (and we beheld his glory, the glory as of the only begotten of the Father), full of grace and truth. (John 1:1–3, 14, KJV, emphasis added)

All things were made by Him: the 137,000,000 light-sensitive cells of your eyes, your information-processing brain, the bones and blood that make up your body. Your ability to have the thoughts you are thinking as you read these words was created by Him. These realities may be mind-boggling to us, but they are totally hidden from this world. Unbelievers don't know who He is, and the thought of His second coming is understandably mocked:

Scoffers will come in the last days, walking according to their own lusts, and saying, "Where is the promise of His coming? For since the fathers fell asleep, all things continue as they were from the beginning of creation." For this they willfully forget: that by the word of God the heavens were of old, and the earth standing out of water and in the water, by which the world that then existed perished, being flooded with water. But the heavens and the earth which are now preserved by the same word, are reserved for fire until the day of judgment and perdition of ungodly men. But, beloved, do not forget this one thing, that with the Lord one day is as a thousand years, and a thousand years as one day. The Lord is not slack concerning His promise, as some count slackness, but is longsuffering toward us, not willing that any should perish but that all should come to repentance. (2 Pet. 3:3–10)

Jesus, once a little babe in a manger, is coming again. That gentle Jesus, meek and mild, the harmless Lamb, is coming back as a lion, and this time He will shake the heavens and the earth

when the Lord Jesus is revealed from heaven with His mighty angels, in flaming fire taking vengeance on those who do not know God, and on those who do not obey the gospel of our Lord Jesus Christ. These shall be punished with everlasting destruction from the presence of the Lord and from the glory of His power, when He comes, in that Day, to be glorified in His saints and to be admired among all those who believe, because our testimony among you was believed. (2 Thess. 1:7–10)

Human beings are the willing mouthpieces for demons to hiss out their hatred of Jesus. They not only mock Him; they also give Him the dubious honor of being the only human being in history to have His name used as a cuss word. Not even Hitler was despised enough to have his name used in such a way. Only Jesus—the One who was given a holy name that is above all names, who is to be called wonderful:

> For unto us a Child is born,
> Unto us a Son is given;
> And the government will be upon His shoulder.
> And His name will be called
> Wonderful, Counselor, Mighty God,
> Everlasting Father, Prince of Peace. (Isa. 9:6)

The one whose name will cause every knee to bow:

At the name of Jesus every knee should bow, of those in heaven, and of those on earth, and of those under the earth. (Phil. 2:10)

Keep this commandment without spot, blameless until our Lord Jesus Christ's appearing, which He will manifest in His own time, He who is the blessed and only Potentate, the King of kings and Lord of lords. (1 Tim. 6:14–15)

Look closely at the following portion of Scripture to see what Jesus said about His deity:

When Jesus came into the region of Caesarea Philippi, He asked His disciples, saying, "Who do men say that I, the Son of Man, am?"

So they said, "Some say John the Baptist, some Elijah, and others Jeremiah or one of the prophets."

He said to them, "But who do you say that I am?"

Simon Peter answered and said, "You are the Christ, the Son of the living God."

Jesus answered and said to him, "Blessed are you, Simon Bar-Jonah, for flesh and blood has not revealed this to you, but My Father who is in heaven." (Matt. 16:14–17)

In other words, it isn't our task to try to convince blind sinners of the identity of Jesus. It takes revelation from the Father Himself. We are simply to preach the everlasting gospel and trust God to guide that arrow to the heart.

While some may feel it is their duty to intellectually convince the world, you remain focused and keep it simple. In doing so you are in good company: "Then I saw another angel flying in the midst of heaven, having the everlasting gospel to preach to those who dwell on the earth—to every nation, tribe, tongue, and people" (Rev. 14:6).

When you preach or witness, always head for the cross—always. Exalt the Savior. Make demons tremble. Preach Jesus. Show the sinful world Christ crucified, and say with the apostle Paul, "I determined not to know anything among you except Jesus Christ and Him crucified" (1 Cor. 2:2).

SIX

Prepared

The Evil Day

Therefore put on the full armor of God, so that when the day of evil comes, you may be able to stand your ground, and after you have done everything, to stand.

Ephesians 6:13 NIV

The *Amplified Bible* renders Ephesians 6:13 this way: "Therefore, put on the complete armor of God, so that you will be able to [successfully] resist and stand your ground in the evil day [of danger], and having done everything [that the crisis demands], to stand firm [in your place, fully prepared, immovable, victorious]."

The dictionary defines a *crisis* as "a time of intense difficulty or danger; . . . a time when a difficult or important decision must be made."[1] While we may prepare ourselves mentally for such times, they tend to arrive unannounced, unexpected, and unplanned. Take, for example, an incident that happened in April 2017:

> Oh boy. A video released by the US Forest Service shows the moment when a gender reveal party in Arizona went horribly wrong, sparking a wildfire that burned nearly 47,000 acres and caused more than $8 million in damage.
>
> Shot on April 23, 2017, the clip shows a makeshift target with the words "Boy" and "Girl" written on it, placed in the middle of the desert near Green Valley, Arizona, south of Tucson.
>
> Seconds later we hear a gunshot, and the target explodes, revealing a blue cloud and immediately igniting the surrounding brush. Someone shouts, "Start packing up!"
>
> The flames spread to the nearby Coronado National Forest, where they became the Sawmill Fire and burned 46,991 acres owned by the state of Arizona, federal agencies and private landowners. Firefighters from at least 20 agencies fought the fire for about a week, according to CNN affiliate KGUN-TV.
>
> The man who shot the target, off-duty US Border Patrol agent Dennis Dickey, pleaded guilty in September of this year to a misdemeanor violation of US Forest Service regulations and was sentenced to five years' probation. He also was ordered to pay $8,188,069 in restitution, starting with an initial payment of $100,000 and monthly payments thereafter.[2]

Sin often starts with something seemingly innocent—just a look, a little lust. Almost everyone does it; it's no more than a tiny spark of pleasure in a dark and depressing world. I know, because I often enjoyed its glow in my BC days. Lust meant instant pleasure, and even after many years of sanctification, there are still warm embers. But I know that those embers can start an out-of-control explosion that could cost me dearly. So I do my best to be prepared. I don't want to get caught unprepared the way that King David was.

Lust's little twinkle promised David pleasure but eventually brought persistent pain. Let me tell you about an *evil day* in David's life. He should have been in battle with his troops instead of walking on his housetop with a wandering eye.

> It happened in the spring of the year, at the time when kings go out to battle, that David sent Joab and his servants with him, and all Israel; and they destroyed the people of Ammon and besieged Rabbah. But David remained at Jerusalem.
>
> Then it happened one evening that David arose from his bed and walked on the roof of the king's house. And from the roof he saw a woman bathing, and the woman was very beautiful to behold. So David sent and inquired about the woman. And someone said, "Is this not Bathsheba, the daughter of Eliam, the wife of Uriah the Hittite?" Then David sent messengers, and took her; and she came to him, and he lay with her, for she was cleansed from her impurity; and she returned to her house. And the woman conceived; so she sent and told David, and said, "I am with child." (2 Sam. 11:1–5)

David was around fifty years old when this happened. He was already into his fortieth year of the seventy-year itch. Lust never leaves a man alone. David should have known that the devil is more than willing to scratch that itch.

You and I must be prepared for our own evil day. We must be in the battle with our troops, fully clothed with the armor of God, so that we can stand firm in the faith and resist the devil.

Judas Iscariot

Judas failed in *his* evil day. It began with temptation. A tiny spark of covetousness entered his sinful heart. He was an idolater. He had no fear of God before his eyes and stole money from the disciples: "But one of His disciples, Judas Iscariot, Simon's son, who would betray Him, said, 'Why was this fragrant oil not sold for three hundred denarii and given to the poor?' This he said, not that he cared for the poor, but because he was a thief, and had the money box; and he used to take what was put in it" (John 12:5–6).

Did he really think he would get away with it? He actually stole from Jesus, and that seemingly small theft gave license to the evil one. It wasn't a big deal at first. But the fire then began to spread until it was out of control. This verse has to be one of the most fearful in Scripture: "Then Satan entered Judas, surnamed Iscariot, who was numbered among the twelve" (Luke 22:3).

Judas gave place to the devil. He neither submitted to God nor resisted the devil, so the devil didn't flee from him (see James 4:7). Instead, he entered the open door and used Judas for his evil purposes—to kill, steal, and destroy. Then came more fire. He killed Judas through suicide and stole his soul. All because of the tiny spark of sin.

Think of what happened to Judas. Jesus chose Judas to follow Him. He rubbed shoulders with Peter, John, Andrew, and the other disciples. But he also fellowshiped with Jesus of Nazareth—God in human form. While multitudes pressed in just to touch Him, Judas was a privileged disciple who ate meals with Him. Judas saw what the prophets of old longed to see—the sick healed, the dead raised, bread and fish multiplied, storms calmed, water walked upon—and still sin deceived him. He fell on the evil day because he had a covetous chink in his armor. His lack of preparation was recorded in Scripture for our admonition. Are we admonished by it? Are we learning the lesson? Search your soul for secret sin. What unlawful box is tempting you? Is the chink in your armor hidden pride, lust, or greed? Here's a partial laundry list:

> Now the works of the flesh are evident, which are: adultery, fornication, uncleanness, lewdness, idolatry, sorcery, hatred, contentions, jealousies, outbursts of wrath, selfish ambitions, dissensions, heresies, envy, murders, drunkenness, revelries, and the like; of which I tell you beforehand, just as I also told you in time past, that those who practice such things will not inherit the kingdom of God. (Gal. 5:19–21)

Taking up the whole armor of God enables us not only to prepare for the evil day but having "done everything, to stand." That means not only to stand our ground in battle but also to *take* ground and hold it. We are not to fall back. To lose zeal for the lost is to fall back. To let fear have its way is to fall back. We are in a war, and in that war, we can have no rest.

C. H. Spurgeon says:

> He only is a true conqueror, and shall be crowned at the last, who continues till war's trumpet is blown no more. Perseverance is, therefore, the target of all our spiritual enemies. The world does not object to your being a Christian for a time, if she can but tempt you to cease your pilgrimage and settle

down to buy and sell with her in Vanity Fair. The flesh will seek to ensnare you, and to prevent your pressing on to glory.

"It is weary work being a pilgrim; come, give it up. Am I always to be mortified? Am I never to be indulged? Give me at least a furlough from this constant warfare."

Satan will make many a fierce attack on your perseverance; it will be the mark for all his arrows. He will strive to hinder you in service: he will insinuate that you are doing no good; and that you want rest. He will endeavor to make you weary of suffering, he will whisper,

"Curse God, and die."

Or he will attack your steadfastness:

"What is the good of being so zealous? Be quiet like the rest; sleep as do others, and let your lamp go out as the other virgins do."

Or he will assail your doctrinal sentiments:

"Why do you hold to these denominational creeds? Sensible men are getting more liberal; they are removing the old landmarks: fall in with the times."

Wear your shield, Christian, therefore, close upon your amour, and cry mightily unto God, that by His Spirit you may endure to the end.[3]

Let me reiterate what Spurgeon said: wear your shield. You must be prepared to be effective and to stand firm against the many evil days that Satan will orchestrate in your life.

Disarming Satan

One of my life's great joys is my lasting friendship with Kirk Cameron. Kirk and I cohosted fifty-two episodes of *The Way of the Master,* an award-winning television program that aired in over 190 countries. In October 2018, I was honored to be a guest on his new TV program, "One to One."

During filming, he told me that he had a surprise for me. In all our previous filming, Kirk had given me only one rule: no surprises. He needed to know what was coming up. Now, *he had a surprise for me . . .* which he revealed *during* the taping. He knew that I had been beaten up once or twice while open-air preaching, and he was taking me to a self-defense course.

I learned a lot that day. I learned lessons that could save my life. One lesson was what to do if someone points a gun at you close range. You don't grab the gun, because it may go off and kill you. Instead, you *redirect* the weapon so that it's not pointing at you. That makes sense. I also learned what to say if someone is coming at you with a knife. You yell, "He's got a knife!" Really loud. That alerts everyone around you as to what is happening so that they can either come to your assistance or call the police. Such knowledge can save lives.

Here is something else that needs to be shouted from the housetops: "Satan has a weapon! It's called sin! And he's walking about as a roaring lion, seeking whom he may devour! He came to kill, steal, and destroy, and his favorite weapons are lust and fear!"

If we want to be more than conquerors in Christ, we must have a strategy to disarm Satan. That's what I call being prepared. Preparation is everything.

I'm prepared for my own "evil day" so that I can help strangers prepare for theirs. Squatters in the park and strangers like Bernard and Jerry—humans like any other, all in need of Christ. In need of you and me and our willingness to be prepared.

As I rode through the local park, I saw someone squatting on the ground. He looked Hispanic, about twenty-five years old, with very long, straggly hair that appeared to have not seen a brush for a long time. He was having breakfast, and it looked like there had been a mini tornado around him. My first thought was that he was demonically possessed. He had the Legion look.

But as I interviewed him, I imagined him in the future. I saw him as a clean-cut, Christ-centered pastor, talking to his flock about how he once sat in a park looking like Charles Manson and heard the gospel for the first time. I saw the bullfrog as a handsome prince.

One of the best ways to prepare for evangelism is to make a habit of seeing sinners as saints. Look at every Saul of Tarsus as an apostle Paul and every prodigal as a restored son, clothed in the garment of righteousness. Faith can do that. It can move mountains.

We can't help but rush to make judgments based on the information we have. But not having all the details can lead us to a wrong conclusion. Such was the case with a man named Bernard. He was in his late thirties and was working out really early one Friday morning in the local park.

I approached him with a friendly, "Good morning. How would you like to do an interview on YouTube?" He was very polite but declined, saying that his wife would go crazy if he came on camera. He looked as though he was from Fiji or perhaps Tonga, so I asked him where he was from. If he was from one of those islands, I could talk about rugby. But I was wrong. He was from Africa.

I asked him why his wife would go crazy if he came on camera. He said that she was on YouTube all the time and wouldn't like to see him there. I said, "Are you a man or a mouse? Tell her that you did an interview, you enjoyed it, and she will enjoy watching it."

He replied, "You don't understand, sir. I'm from Africa. I'm not yet an American citizen, and she just may kick me out."

That information changed my perspective. He wasn't being a mouse; he was being a wise old owl. I said, "I totally understand. . . . May I talk to you without the camera for a few minutes?" He said he was reluctant, so I jumped in before he declined and asked if he thought he was a good person. He said there is not a good person on the face of the earth. What he said was very biblical, so I asked if he was a Christian. He replied that he wasn't but his parents were.

I took him through the Commandments and into the grace of the gospel, and he was very receptive. But when I told him that he needed to get right with God today, he said he would repent at the last minute of his life. I told him that he may not get a last minute and that we're talking about his eternity.

I knew it was time to wrap things up. "Bernard, I've got a gift for you. Is that okay?" I asked him.

"What if I don't take it?"

I replied, "Then you will miss out," and handed him Subway and movie gift cards.

"Why are you doing this?" he asked.

I told him that it was because I loved him. "Here's one for your wife too," I added.

"Why are you doing this?" he asked a second time.

Again, I said it was because I loved him and cared about where he would spend eternity. He kept saying, "This has made my day. I don't deserve this." Then he began to ask questions about our movies. When I asked, "Do you have a Bible?" he said that he did. And when I said, "Well, dust it off," he answered, "Yes sir, I'll dust it off."

I met Jerry as he was ending a workout in the park. He had been running, and his brow was covered with sweat. I was almost certain that he wouldn't want to be bothered to come on camera. But to my delight, with a little coaxing, he said he would do an interview.

Jerry was probably in his early thirties, had a deep rich voice, and stood six feet, four inches tall. He stood in the parking lot, and I stood on a raised sidewalk. I asked my first question—*Had he ever given thought to the big questions such as the purpose of life and what happens after we die?* He said that he had given both those questions much thought. When I asked if he had come up with an answer, he said in a tone of frustration that he hadn't. He added that perhaps we are reincarnated, but he didn't know. When I asked who he thought was in charge of giving out bodies in the reincarnation process, Jerry thought that *we* are the ones who choose what body we want. I asked him jokingly if he would like to come back as a butterfly, and he smiled and added a sad, "I don't think I would bother coming back."

His choice not to live again made sense for an unsaved person. The pleasures of life are not worth the pain. After all, multitudes choose death by suicide to escape their pain. Not choosing to come back to life would be a simple and painless escape. It made me wonder how many people, if given the option, would have chosen not to be born.

But the good thing about Jerry's hopelessness was that it left him honest, humble, and very open to the gospel. Yet, he wasn't anxious about his salvation. We long to hear sinners say, "*What must I do to be saved!?*" Those were the words of the Philippian jailer who had just experienced a prison-shaking earthquake—that he mistakenly thought had emptied his jail of all its prisoners. That suddenly left him in a horrible dilemma, because Roman law said he would have to suffer the sentence of any prisoners who escaped. He would certainly have been executed. He was helpless and hopeless in the face of Roman law, and the sinner who is suddenly awakened sees himself as helpless and hopeless in the face of God's law, awaiting certain execution. But Jerry wasn't like the Philippian jailer. Maybe he will be some day, but I won't get to see it. I was consoled by the fact that Jerry finally *did* see his dilemma, and he assured me that he would give his salvation some serious thought.

His sobering words about not wanting to come back to life stayed with me. He made me think about how painful life is for so many. I thought about a couple who had befriended my family when we first came to the United States back in 1989. They must have taken us out to dinner a hundred times in the following years, and never once would they let us pay. Not only that, but they sent our whole family Christmas presents for many years. Even though circumstances had caused us to drift apart, we loved that couple and were deeply saddened when we heard that the husband had died of cancer, leaving his dear wife, Debbie, utterly broken. Without the hope of the gospel, life would have been nothing but a hopeless nightmare for her. During the same period of time, my faithful producer found out that his eldest son had been in a serious car accident and was in the hospital in critical condition with suspected brain damage. The thought that multitudes throughout the world today will wake up to similar nightmares overwhelms me, and even more so when you add to that the hopelessness of their unrepentant state. Even though the thought is almost suffocating, it should spur us on to prepare well and fearlessly reach out to the lost. We can give them the hope that they so desperately need.

SEVEN

Truthful

What the Gospel Is Not

> Stand therefore, having girded your waist with truth, having
> put on the breastplate of righteousness.
>
> Ephesians 6:14

Three times in Ephesians 6:13–14 we are told to stand. The third use of *stand* is directly followed by the word *therefore*. In other words, there is a *reason* we are to stand our ground. We are to stand with our waists girded with truth and our breastplates of righteousness on so that when the evil day comes we can stand for the truth of the gospel. The gospel and the truth cannot be separated. They are so intertwined that "gospel" and "truth" are synonymous in our language. Look at the etymology of the following idioms:

Gospel truth: "Something that is unquestionably true. *For example, Every word he uttered was the gospel truth.* The word *gospel*, which comes from the Old English *god spel*, 'good news,' has been used to describe something that is thought to be as true as the biblical gospel (that is, undeniably true) since the 13th century. The current idiom originated in the 1600s, when it referred to biblical truths, and has been applied to truth of a more general nature since the late 1800s."[1]

Take as gospel: "Also, take for gospel. Believe absolutely, regard as true, as in *We took every word of his as gospel, but in fact he was often mistaken.* This idiom, first recorded in 1496, uses *gospel* in the sense of the absolute truth."[2]

Our language makes these nods to the understanding that *gospel* means "truth," even though our culture denies it. The enemy has made certain of that. The reason we are to make a stand for truth is that the enemy stands for the opposite. He is the father of lies—the supreme and subtle serpent of deception that has deceived many by poisoning the message. The subtlety is that the poisoned gospel is still called good news, but it is not.

If we are going to speak the truth in love, we must make sure that we're speaking the truth. The good news we are to herald is that Christ died for our sins and rose again on the third day. If we preach that His suffering wasn't sufficient (and that we, therefore, have to add our works to it), we poison the message. It kills rather than makes alive. And the gospel we preach becomes *another* gospel—a false news.

This problem has been around much longer than we have. People in the church in Galatia taught that the work of the cross fell short as the means of salvation and that believers, therefore, needed to keep the moral law. But look at Paul's scathing rebuke:

> I marvel that you are turning away so soon from Him who called you in the grace of Christ, to a different gospel, which is not another; but there are some who trouble you and want to pervert the gospel of Christ. But even if we, or an angel from heaven, preach any other gospel to you than what we have preached to you, let him be accursed. As we have said before, so now I say again, if anyone preaches any other gospel to you than what you have received, let him be accursed. (Gal. 1:6–9)

Paul says we should be cursed by God if we teach that our works must be added to Christ's work on the cross. But this is the poisonous teaching of cults and other institutions that claim to be Christian in doctrine. A gospel of salvation by works is not Christian. Paul begins his rebuke with "I marvel that you are turning away so soon from Him who called you in the grace of Christ." We are called in the *grace* of Christ. Grace cannot be earned. It is unmerited: "For by grace you have been saved through faith, and that not of yourselves; it is the gift of God, not of works, lest anyone should boast" (Eph. 2:8–9).

I was on the pier at Huntington Beach on a very windy day when I stopped a couple and asked them for an interview. When I said I wanted to know what they thought happened after death, the man turned to his wife and said, "You are into Bahá'í . . . do it."

We found a place out of the wind, and she launched into the story of how she had almost died while hospitalized for a rare respiratory disease. Death came so close that three times her family called for a Catholic priest. But God had mercy on her, and here she was, alive and kicking. She said that in a near-death experience, her dead relatives had appeared at her bedside.

After she recovered, she turned to the Bahá'í religion. I let her talk for some time. She had a zeal for it that shamed most Christians. Then I preached Christ crucified, covering the law before sharing the gospel.

As we were concluding, she said that the Bahá'í believed Jesus was a prophet. As gently as I could, I told her that Hitler believed in Jesus too, but it was a *different* Jesus. The Mormons also have a different Jesus; theirs is Lucifer's brother. If we have a different Jesus, we will have a different gospel. I explained again that she needed to repent and trust in the *biblical* Jesus. This is the One who suffered *once* for sin (see 1 Pet. 3:18), the One who said, "It is finished" (see John 19:28–30). I wanted this woman to embrace the Savior as Lord and therefore obey His words, not the sayings of a Jesus inspired by the father of lies.

The Big Curveball

Life is like one big curveball. We can strike out at any moment. We simply don't know what each day will bring.

It's traditional for the older generation to talk about how difficult things were in their youth. I'm going to carry on this tradition. As a teenager, I rode a bike three miles to school every day. We lived by the ocean, and each night the air would cool down. That meant there would be a wind blowing off-shore in the morning. Each morning, I had a headwind for my three-mile ride inland to school. Then, almost every day, the sun would heat up the land and the air would rise and bring in an onshore breeze—which meant I had a headwind for the three-mile ride home as well.

Life is like that. The winds of adversity blow against us almost daily. For the Christian, it builds the muscle of character. But for the non-Christian, life can feel like nothing but an ongoing battle of futility. If that sounds like an exaggeration, consider the fact that every year about half a million Americans end up in the hospital as a result of suicide attempts. Look at this alarming article titled "Suicide, at 50-Year Peak, Pushes Down US Life Expectancy":

> Suicides and drug overdoses pushed up U.S. deaths last year, and drove a continuing decline in how long Americans are expected to live.
>
> Overall, there were more than 2.8 million U.S. deaths in 2017, or nearly 70,000 more than the previous year, the Centers for Disease Control and Prevention said Thursday. It was the most deaths in a single year since the government began counting more than a century ago.
>
> The increase partly reflects the nation's growing and aging population. But it's deaths in younger age groups—particularly middle-aged people—that have had the largest impact on calculations of life expectancy, experts said.
>
> "These sobering statistics are a wake-up call that we are losing too many Americans, too early and too often, to conditions that are preventable," Dr. Robert Redfield, the CDC's director, said in a statement.[3]

The CDC did not speculate about what's behind the decline, but Dr. William Dietz, a disease prevention expert at George Washington University, "sees a sense of hopelessness. . . . I really do believe that people are increasingly hopeless, and that that leads to drug use; it leads potentially to suicide."[4]

There is no true hope outside of the gospel. Every other hope is dashed by the reality of death. It is the final and ultimate storm. If our house is built on rock, we will stand. If it's not, we will crumble. And millions crumble. They turn to drugs, alcohol, or suicide, and some lose their minds. But there is hope, even for those who seem to have already crumbled. There is a *rock* foundation that can save them from devastation. Jesus said of Himself, "Therefore whoever hears these sayings of Mine, and does them, I will liken him to a wise man who built his house on the rock" (Matt. 7:24).

Our agenda is to point sinners to the Savior and His words. We want them to see their sin, see the cross, and yield to His lordship. We use the law to bring the knowledge of sin. Scripture says it is a "tutor *to bring us to Christ*" (Gal. 3:24, emphasis added). The law directs us to the biblical Jesus. The law leaves us dying of thirst in a desert where only One is saying, "If anyone thirsts, let [them] come to me and drink" (John 7:37). We must present the gospel of grace and not "another gospel" or "another Jesus." C. H. Spurgeon says:

> Now, that faith which unites to the Lamb is an instantaneous gift of God, and he who believes on the Lord Jesus is that moment saved, without anything else whatsoever. Ah! my friends, do we not want more exalting Christ in our

preaching, and more exalting Christ in our living? Poor Mary said, "They have taken away my Lord and I know not where they have laid him." And she might say so now-a-days if she could rise from the grave. Oh! to have a Christ-exalting ministry! Oh! to have preaching that magnifies Christ in his person, that extols his divinity, that loves his humanity; to have preaching that shows him as prophet, priest, and king to his people! to have preaching whereby the spirit manifests the Son of God unto his children: to have preaching that says, "Look unto him and be ye saved all the ends of the earth,"—Calvary preaching, Calvary theology, Calvary books, Calvary sermons! These are the things we want, and in proportion as we have Calvary exalted and Christ magnified, the gospel is preached in our midst.[5]

Paul admonishes us to stand strong against error, declaring the truth of God's Word at all times:

> I charge you therefore before God and the Lord Jesus Christ, who will judge the living and the dead at His appearing and His kingdom: Preach the word! Be ready in season and out of season. Convince, rebuke, exhort, with all longsuffering and teaching. For the time will come when they will not endure sound doctrine, but according to their own desires, because they have itching ears, they will heap up for themselves teachers; and they will turn their ears away from the truth, and be turned aside to fables. But you be watchful in all things, endure afflictions, do the work of an evangelist, fulfill your ministry. (2 Tim. 4:1–4)

We are charged to stand strong, guarding the truth, because there is going to be a day of wrath when God will judge the living and the dead. Paul is passionate: "Preach the word! Be ready in season and out of season."

This isn't preaching from the pulpit to the choir. *It is a pleading with the unsaved*, those who are still in their sins and face judgment when Christ returns.

We *convince* them with the law of their terrible danger. We *rebuke* them because they have gone astray and turned others to their way. And then we *exhort* them with the gospel. We plead with them to lay down their weapons and look to God for mercy. And we do so with the tears of *long-suffering*. We must never let our frustration with the blind manifest anger. We must refrain from the desire to scream at the lost, "*What is wrong with you?* God is offering you everlasting life, and you're looking at your watch! The time will come when time overtakes you, and the grim reaper falls on you, and you scream for mercy to the Judge, but He will only have wrath left for you."

Truth doesn't scream because it doesn't have to. Truth—only the one gospel truth—will lead sinners to Jesus. We are to stand in the truth and preach it. The rest is up to God.

The Catalyst for Evangelism

Let's consider the exhortation in Ephesians 6:14 again: "Stand therefore, having girded your waist with truth, having put on the breastplate of righteousness." If we stand in the truth, we're standing up for God's righteousness. We know that the righteousness spoken of here is not the outward righteousness of those who are merely religious. It is

110

an inward *heart* righteousness. It is the perfect righteousness demanded by the perfect law of God.

Speaking of perfection, let's talk about my perfect record: if there's milk within a mile, I will spill it. I did as a child, and I still do as an adult. At the 2018 Living Waters Thanksgiving lunch, I wanted to be a servant to our staff. So I offered my help in the kitchen. Someone placed a huge tray covered with tin foil into my hands. I assumed it was a large turkey. I carried the tray down the hallway to the stairs, totally determined not to drop it. If I did, I would never live it down. As I carefully navigated the stairs, I felt something spilling on my shirt and on my pants. Unbeknownst to me, it was not a turkey I was carrying but a large semicarved ham, sitting in a pool of warm and fatty juice, most of which was now soaked into my pants and the lower half of my shirt. It looked disgusting. My appearance brought unsurprised smiles to the staff members who were waiting for dinner in our dining room.

When I said that I was going home to change, many of the staffers encouraged me to stay as I was, saying that I looked fine. I knew better. No one looks fine when they're covered in pig juice.

Many so-called Christians encourage the unsaved to stay as they are. They think they look fine. God is loving and kind. He's not mad at anybody, so there won't be a judgment day, let alone a literal hell. These "stay-as-you-are" Christians don't see God as righteous. Paul speaks of Israel's ignorance of God's nature: "Brethren, my heart's desire and prayer to God for Israel is that they may be saved. For I bear them witness that they have a zeal for God, but not according to knowledge. For they being ignorant of God's righteousness, and seeking to establish their own righteousness, have not submitted to the righteousness of God" (Rom. 10:1–3).

If God *isn't* perfectly righteous, then we are fine—even if covered in pig juice! There is no wrath, no hell, and no need of the Savior. But the world doesn't understand that the long arm of the law reaches right down into the human heart.

Many Jews I've spoken with believe all is well because they think the Old Testament makes no mention of hell—but it does. Here is a sampling:

For a fire is kindled in My anger, and shall burn unto the lowest hell; it shall consume the earth with her increase, and set on fire the foundations of the mountains. (Deut. 32:22)

The sorrows of hell compassed me about; the snares of death [confronted] me. (2 Sam. 22:6 KJV)

The wicked shall be turned into hell, and all the nations that forget God. (Ps. 9:17)

For great is thy mercy toward me: and thou hast delivered my soul from the lowest hell. (Ps. 86:13 KJV)

The sorrows of death compassed me, and the pains of hell [got] hold upon me: I found trouble and sorrow. (Ps. 116:3 KJV)

If I ascend into heaven, You are there; if I make my bed in hell, behold, You are there. (Ps. 139:8)

But he does not know that the dead are there, that her guests are in the depths of hell. (Prov. 9:18)

Hell and destruction are before the LORD; so how much more the hearts of the [children] of men? (Prov. 15:11)

The way of life winds upward for the wise, that [they] may turn away from hell below. (Prov. 15:24)

Hell and destruction are never full; so the eyes of [humans] are never satisfied. (Prov. 27:20)

Hell from beneath is excited about you, to meet you at your coming; it stirs up the dead for you, all the chief ones of the earth; it has raised up from their thrones all the kings of the nations. (Isa. 14:9)

People across the world from all cultures and groups don't believe in hell because they are "ignorant of God's righteousness, and seeking to establish their own righteousness." Those who are ignorant of the law are ignorant of the necessity of righteousness. To them, the existence of hell seems unreasonable. But to the people who understand righteousness, the existence of hell is inevitable. The moral law reveals that God demands absolute moral perfection. Therefore, the reality of hell is the catalyst for evangelism.

"Therefore go into the highways, and as many as you find, invite to the wedding." So those servants went out into the highways and gathered together all whom they found, both bad and good. And the wedding hall was filled with guests.

But when the king came in to see the guests, he saw a man there who did not have on a wedding garment. So he said to him, "Friend, how did you come in here without a wedding garment?" And he was speechless. Then the king said to the servants, "Bind him hand and foot, take him away, and cast him into outer darkness; there will be weeping and gnashing of teeth." (Matt. 22:9–13)

How my heart breaks because sinners are deceived into thinking that a pure and holy God will accept pig juice slopped over the garments of sinners. So many show signs of contempt and impatience when I tell them that Jesus can make them clean. They will curse the day they showed such disdain for the gospel. They didn't see their need for a white robe: "Then a white robe was given to each of them; and it was said to them that they should rest a little while longer, until both the number of their fellow servants and their brethren, who would be killed as they were, was completed" (Rev. 6:11).

We, on the other hand, "having girded [our] waist with truth," wear our wedding robes proudly, calling out to others to come and join the feast.

The Dragon Slayer

We need the truth of the moral law to slay the dragon of self-righteousness in sinners. I spoke to a man named Steve (and his wife) through the window of their car. Even after hearing the truth of salvation by grace alone, he tried to hold on to the thought that we are to give God little sacrifices.

Steve believed in an afterlife and in God as a higher power. When I asked "Do you think He is happy with you?" he replied that when he did certain things he was rewarded. He also admitted that some things he did displeased God.

When I asked for specifics, Steve simply said that God wasn't happy when he wasn't being himself. He spoke of sacrificing himself for the needs of others, saying that was when he usually felt the most rewarded. But when I asked him if he was a good person, he revealed that his philosophy wasn't really working. He said, "That's hard to say. And I fear the day when I am judged. It's frightening."

Scripture addresses Steve's philosophy in this way: "How much more shall the blood of Christ, who through the eternal Spirit offered Himself without spot to God, cleanse your conscience from dead works to serve the living God?" (Heb. 9:14).

Steve's attempts to balance the scales with his sacrificial good works still left him with a conscience that accused him of sin and produced guilt, which in turn incited fear of judgment. His works were "dead" works. They can't do anything for him. The only thing that can cleanse his conscience is the blood of Christ. It was shed to redeem us from the curse of the law.

When I asked Steve if he had kept the Ten Commandments, he said he had broken a couple. He had lied and stolen in his younger years. He explained these away, as many other unsaved individuals have done when I've talked to them. When people don't understand the gospel, they try to justify themselves. They attempt to cover their sins. This is typically done by saying that the sins were committed in the past and weren't serious.

I took Steve through six of the Ten Commandments. When I asked him if he would be innocent or guilty on the day of judgment, he said, "Hopefully, I would be absolved from all my sins, but I would be guilty. . . . I would probably end up going to hell." Then he said, "But my outlook is that for a couple of times in life that you do wrong, you make it up with all the good doing in the rest of your life."

I told Steve to imagine himself being in a court of law, having committed a very serious crime, like robbing a bank and shooting a guard on his way out. The judge would say that Steve was guilty, to which he would agree. Then, I asked him to imagine defending himself with the statement he had just made to me.

"Your good deeds have nothing to do with your crime," I told him. "A judge will judge you only on the crimes you've committed. And it is exactly the same with God." When I asked him how he could be absolved of his sins, he responded that he hoped he would be forgiven through the cross. I agreed and then explained the gospel, saying that Jesus paid the fine in full so that his case could be dismissed.

I told Steve what he had to do was repent and trust in God alone. He was like a man who was going to jump ten thousand feet out of a plane with no parachute and planning to flap his arms to save himself. Steve's wife was nodding and smiling in agreement. I said, "Give up trying to save yourself and trust the parachute."

As our conversation concluded, he spoke of us giving ourselves to God as a sacrifice. While, as Christians, we are to present our bodies as living sacrifices for His service, we initially come to the cross with nothing in our hands, *because the sacrifice has already been made.* Even when someone has all the right words, such as *absolve* and *sacrifice*, they can still be far away from the truth. It's our job to point them back to the truth at every opportunity.

Let me give you one final word on presenting the truth to a world that doesn't want to hear it: it takes courage. And that courage is built over time.

Perhaps as you have read about how I approach strangers, you've been impressed. But you shouldn't be. I've now done it so many times that it no longer takes much courage. If *you* give out your first gospel tract and it terrifies you, you are a far greater warrior than me. Would you be impressed if you heard that a billionaire gave twenty dollars to a charity? I don't think so. It would likely make you angry. But if you heard that a six-year-old gave twenty dollars from their allowance that had taken months to save, *that* would be impressive. It would bring tears to your eyes.

So be encouraged—approaching your very first stranger is impressive. Don't let fear define or confine you. Stand against the methods of the enemy. Stand in the truth of the gospel. And having done all, stand.

EIGHT

Practiced

What Are You Preaching?

Having shod your feet with the preparation of the gospel
of peace.

Ephesians 6:15

If you've been paying any attention at all, you know that
Sam is my dog. Both he and I wear sunglasses on our bike
rides. He sits on a platform I made especially for him, and
he gets more attention than the presidential motorcade. I
was on my bike, on my way to share the gospel, when a
man in his midfifties turned a corner and walked down our
street. The man was just a few feet in front of me, so I came
alongside him and asked, "How you doing?" As he stared
at Sam, I followed up with, "What's your name?" He said it
was Mitch. "Mitch, are you reading your Bible?" I asked. He
replied that he hadn't been lately, so I added, "Don't forget

your Creator because you don't know when you're going to die." He said, "I wish I had my camera!"

Mitch, like many of the people I meet, was clearly more interested in a dog wearing sunglasses than in his own eternal salvation. I told him, "Jesus said that whoever looks on a woman in lust for her has committed adultery already with her in his heart. *That's* how high God's standard will be on judgment day. That's why you need to trust in Jesus to save you. Okay?"

Mitch replied, "Thanks, much appreciated," and we parted ways. All that happened in about forty seconds.

I was able to speak to him because I was ready. I was prepared. I had *practiced* what I was going to preach. The gun was in the holster. The bullets were in the gun. My waiting hand was twitching. The arrows were in the bow! The cannon was loaded. The metaphors are overkill, but you get my point.

Could you do what I did? You won't be able to unless you have your feet shod with the *preparation* of the gospel of peace. Are you always ready? If not, practice what you preach. Prepare yourself so that you are always ready to share something that could cause the lost to seek after God and trust in the Savior. If we fail to plan, we plan to fail.

In 1 Peter 3:15, we are admonished to *always* be prepared to preach the gospel: "But sanctify the Lord God in your hearts, and always be ready to give a defense to everyone who asks you a reason for the hope that is in you, with meekness and fear."

Here is the same verse in the (slightly louder) *Amplified Bible*: "But in your hearts set Christ apart [as holy—acknowledging Him, giving Him first place in your lives] as

Lord. Always be ready to give a [logical] defense to anyone who asks you to account for the hope and confident assurance [elicited by faith] that is within you, yet [do it] with gentleness and respect."

If Jesus has top priority in my life and His will comes before mine, my fear of rejection doesn't matter. It doesn't even come into the equation. If we have our shoes on, we will always be ready to run toward His will.

We take shoes for granted, but if you've ever found yourself walking barefoot on a sandy beach on a hot day, you will understand what purpose shoes fulfill. Having your feet shod with preparation will take the heat out of witnessing.

When it comes to witnessing, I have found that I am either my worst enemy or my best friend. I can side with my loveless flesh or discipline myself to ignore it. If I go into a store to buy something and don't *determine* ahead of time to give out tracts in the store, I won't. So I do myself a huge favor. I place the tracts in my hand before I walk in the front door—the right way up, ready to give out. Typically, I use our very popular Million Dollar Bill tracts. Keeping them in my pocket or holding them upside down can be huge obstacles when I encounter someone. If they are in my pocket, my carnal mind will say, *Aw, that happened quick. That guy looked at me and said hello, but I wasn't quick enough to give him a tract. Too bad.* And then I inwardly smile in relief that I didn't have to confront him and risk rejection. I'm a selfish coward. If I don't let love have its way, I stop caring that people are going to hell. So I hold the tracts in hand ready to go and keep my mind *determined* to ignore fear.

Know Your Weapons

If we are truly practicing, we should know the gospel so that we can preach it to every creature as we have been commanded to do. Paul said, "Woe is me if I do not preach the gospel" (1 Cor. 9:16). He didn't say that about prophecy, water baptism, or biblical apologetics. He warned:

> I marvel that you are turning away so soon from Him who called you in the grace of Christ, to *a different gospel,* which is not another; but there are some who trouble you and want to pervert *the gospel of Christ.* But even if we, or an angel from heaven, preach any other gospel to you than what we have preached to you, let him be accursed. As we have said before, so now I say again, if anyone preaches *any other gospel* to you than what you have received, let him be accursed. (Gal. 1:6–9, emphasis added)

Those who pervert the gospel are damned *because by the gospel sinners come to salvation.* Without the real gospel, sinners go to hell. What, then, could be more important than the gospel? It is the cure to the disease of death. To not preach it is to leave sinners in death's terrible grip.

The word *gospel* simply means "good news." Distilled to its essence, the good news is that Jesus of Nazareth suffered on the cross and rose from the dead three days later. His suffering justifies guilty sinners. If you suddenly learned that you had to jump ten thousand feet out of a plane, and I found a parachute on board and gave it to you, that would be good news. But if you didn't know that you had to jump, the good news would be irrelevant. Therefore, to make you *desire* the parachute, I need to tell you about the jump—*so that the parachute's existence becomes good news to you.*

So it is with the gospel. The gospel is irrelevant foolishness until sinners understand that they must pass through death and face a law they have violated a multitude of times. Charles Spurgeon says:

> Lower the Law and you dim the light by which man perceives his guilt. This is a very serious loss to the sinner rather than a gain, for it lessens the likelihood of his conviction and conversion. . . . I say you have deprived the gospel of its most able auxiliary [its most powerful weapon] when you have set aside the law. You have taken away from it the schoolmaster that is to bring men to Christ. . . . They will never accept grace till they tremble before a just and holy law. Therefore the law serves a most necessary and blessed purpose, and it must not be removed from its place.[1]

If we care about the lost, we must give them the gospel. We may use persuasion and rhetoric and apologetics, but these things are not the power of God for salvation. The *gospel* is. Sinners need to hear the gospel to be saved. Jesus said that the true convert is one who hears and understands (see Matt. 13:23). And this is what the dark forces of this world don't want sinners to understand: "But even if *our gospel* is veiled, it is veiled to those who are perishing, whose minds the god of this age has blinded, who do not believe, lest the light of *the gospel* of the glory of Christ, who is the image of God, should shine on them" (2 Cor. 4:3–4, emphasis added).

Spurgeon expounds our moral obligation from Paul's words: "For though I preach the gospel, I have nothing to glory of: for necessity is laid upon me; yea, woe is unto me, if I preach not the gospel" (1 Cor. 9:16 KJV). He says:

> Put thine ear at hell's gate, and for a little while list to the commingled screams and shrieks of agony and fell despair that shall lend thine ear; and as thou comest from that sad place with that doleful music still affrighting thee, thou wilt hear the voice, "Minister! minister! woe is unto thee if thou preachest not the gospel." Only let us have these things before our eyes, and we must preach. *Stop preaching! Stop preaching!* Let the sun stop shining, and we will preach in darkness. Let the waves stop their ebb and flow, and still our voice shall preach the gospel, let the world stop its revolutions, let the planets stay their motion; we will still preach the gospel. Until the fiery center of this earth shall burst through the thick ribs of her brazen mountains, we shall still preach the gospel; till the universal conflagration shall dissolve the earth, and matter shall be swept away, these lips, or the lips of some others called of God, shall still thunder forth the voice of Jehovah. We cannot help it. "Necessity is laid upon us, yea woe is unto us if we preach not the gospel."[2]

Let's talk about what happens when we don't prepare and practice, and I hope that I'm not misunderstood. I'm going to mention by name a famous Christian brother to make a very important point. I could avoid the topic altogether, but this issue is too important to keep silent about it. This dear man didn't say anything that was wrong or offensive. What he said was good and right. It is what he *didn't* say that I want to highlight. I want to shout what he *didn't* say from the mountaintops, so that no Christian in the future will be unprepared and guilty of this common omission.

Steve Scalise miraculously lived through a shooting in Washington, DC, in 2017. The *New York Times* reported:

> A lone gunman who was said to be distraught over President Trump's election opened fire on members of the Republican congressional baseball team at a practice field in this Washington suburb on Wednesday, using a rifle to shower the field with bullets that struck four people, including Steve Scalise, the majority whip of the House of Representatives.[3]

His amazing return to Congress was given worldwide publicity. Normal programming halted and went live to video feed of Scalise struggling up to the lectern in the House. It was an unprecedented opportunity to give glory to God for being delivered from almost certain death. A friend who knows Steve well told me that he was going to make this speech, and I was very excited as I turned on the TV. Scalise courageously thanked God for delivering him. Following is some of what he said to an audience of hundreds of millions, edited to the parts in which he unashamedly spoke about prayer and God:

> Wow. Thank you, Mr. Speaker.
>
> You have no idea how great this feels to be back here at work in "the People's House." As you can imagine, these last three and a half months have been pretty challenging times for me and my family. But if you look at the outpouring of love, of warmth, of prayer . . it's given us the strength to get through all of this and to get to this point today.

And it starts with God.

For when I was laying out on that ball field, the first thing I did, once I was down and I couldn't move anymore, is I just started to pray. And I'll tell you it gave me an unbelievable sense of calm knowing that at that point it was in God's hands. But I prayed for very specific things. And I will tell you, pretty much every one of those prayers was answered. And they were some pretty challenging prayers I was putting in God's hands. But, He really did deliver for me and my family; and it just gives you that renewed faith and understanding that the power of prayer is something that you just cannot underestimate.

So I'm definitely a living example that miracles really do happen. . . . When I was laying on the ground, one of the things I prayed for is that David and Crystal would be successful in carrying out their duties. . . .

Who would have thought that God would have put Brad out there on the field with me; because the tourniquet he applied, many will tell you, saved my life so that I could actually make it to the hospital in time with all the blood loss. . . .

But what we also saw were prayer groups and well-wishes being given from people that we'd never met before, throughout all of your districts. And you shared it with me. And it was one of those things that was hard for us to completely comprehend—that you had people from all walks of life that had never met me before, and yet they saw what had happened and they just wanted to offer prayers. . . . That warmth and love gave us just incredible strength that you can't imagine during some really, really difficult times. And so that is one more example of the power of prayer. . . .

And the first thing I can tell you is, yes, it changed me, but not in the ways you might think. It's only strengthened my faith in God.[4]

Our dear brother spoke boldly about God, but *he didn't share the gospel*. Read his words again. If you didn't know he was a Christian, his speech wouldn't have informed you of that fact. The same words could have come from the lips of a Muslim who was sincerely thankful for the miracle of deliverance.

Scalise made no mention of the name of Jesus, the glorious cross, the reality of sin, the inevitability of judgment day, the terror of a very real hell, the unspeakably kind offer of everlasting life as the free gift of God, nor of the necessity for the unsaved to repent and trust the Savior. My heart broke, because the sympathetic ears of hundreds of millions were hanging on to his every word.

Some may say that Steve Scalise is a politician, not a professional preacher, and therefore can be excused for failing to preach the gospel. But I'm sure he believes the Bible. I'm sure he knows that those who die in their sins will justly go to a terrifying hell. Should I neglect to sound an alarm because I'm not a professional firefighter? Do I stand and watch a building burn with people inside without calling "Fire!" and alerting them? *Every* Christian is called to the task of evangelism. It is our most basic moral obligation. We must prepare our hearts to warn *everyone* (see Col. 1:28), practice what we preach, and preach what we practice. We must always be ready so that we don't miss the opportunity.

If I'd had the opportunity to speak with the congressman before he addressed Congress, I would have told him he could easily fit the gospel into his testimony of deliverance, just by saying something like this:

> As I lay bleeding on the grass that day, believing that I was about to die, I thanked God that I knew where I was going had death taken me. Jesus took the punishment for my sins when He suffered on the cross. Ten years ago, I looked at the Ten Commandments and realized that I was in big trouble with God come judgment day. Will you go to heaven when you die? Here's a quick test: Have you ever lied, stolen, used God's name in vain, or lusted after a woman? If you have done these things, God sees you as a lying, thieving, blasphemous adulterer at heart, and the Bible warns that one day God will punish you in a terrible place called hell. But He is not willing that any should perish. Sinners broke God's law, and Jesus paid their fine. This means that God can legally dismiss their case: "For God so loved the world that He gave His only begotten Son, that whoever believes in Him should not perish but have everlasting life." Then Jesus rose from the dead, defeating death. Today, repent and trust Jesus, and God will give you eternal life as a free gift. Then read the Bible daily and obey it. God will never fail you. Please think about these things, because none of us know when we are going to die. I'm honored to speak to you. Thank you for your patience and for listening to me.

He would have had the same courtesy of applause, but hundreds of millions would have heard the glorious gospel, and God's Word never returns in vain.

Are you practicing for your own opportunities to share the gospel?

One day you may have the chance to speak into the ears of sinners—perhaps at a packed funeral where your hearers are being reminded of death. In this context, it's thoroughly appropriate for you to tell them how they can live forever.

Perhaps you will be asked to speak at a wedding, where, again, it's thoroughly appropriate to speak of the meaning of marriage—that Christ is the groom, His church is the bride, and we need to be made pure.

Perhaps you will be asked to say something at a birthday celebration, where you could talk about being born again and how Jesus said we all need two birthdays to find everlasting life. If you have a mind to, you will weave the gospel into a celebration of anything—because human beings are going to hell. Therefore, we say with the apostle Paul:

> For though I am free from all [people], I have made myself a servant to all, that I might win the more; and to the Jews I became as a Jew, that I might win Jews; to those who are under the law, as under the law, that I might win those who are under the law; to those who are without law, as without law (not being without law toward God, but under law toward Christ), that I might win those who are without law; to the weak I became as weak, that I might win the weak. I have become all things to all [people], that I might by all means save some. Now this I do for the gospel's sake, that I may be partaker of it with you. (1 Cor. 9:19–23)

I sometimes watch state funerals, when tens of millions will tune in. My hope is that I will hear the gospel. The preacher will instead give the promises of God to the ungodly and eulogize the unsaved deceased as a morally good man rather than a sinner.

If the thought of *preaching* the message I suggested to the Congressman terrifies you, *read* it. Write it down and bring it with you. This is another great way to practice. Just say to your hearers: "I get really nervous in the moment. I'd rather have a root canal. But what I have to say is too important for me to be worried about myself. So I'm going to read it to you."

The gospel is a simple message. We have broken the Commandments, are guilty before the holy God, and are heading for hell. But because God is rich in mercy, He provided a Savior. He commands all people everywhere to repent—because He has appointed a day in which He will judge the world.

Is that so hard to say? It would seem so. The gospel message from modern pulpits is not always clear and simple. It's murky.

If a house was on fire and people were asleep inside, would you give a murky message? Of course not. Your voice would raise the dead. You would make sure they were aware of their danger. If you got into the house and found them sleeping, you would slap their faces to wake them.

The Bible tells us to lift up our voices as trumpets and show all people their transgressions. Yet there is hardly a peep from many pulpits. I suppose this omission comes from a lack of practice. So take heart and get prepared!

Practiced Feet

The Bible says to "be diligent to present yourself approved to God, a worker who does not need to be ashamed" (2 Tim.

2:15). We practice so that we are ready to answer *everyone* who asks us the reason for our faith. Some of the questions asked of us are silly, some are smoke screens, and some are sophisticated. But we should still be ready to answer with patience as many questions as we can because we want to see every mountain brought low and every valley filled. We want sinners to have a straight path to the Lord.

The key to giving sinners answers isn't necessarily being familiar with every question. It's knowing the Scriptures. We are prepared and practiced by knowing sound doctrine. When I was first born again, I remember looking at my Bible and wanting to know every verse. I wanted to understand what God's Word said on every subject. More than forty-five years later, I still don't know every word, but I have practiced my knowledge of sound doctrine.

You know what is crooked *because* you carry a straight ruler with you. The straight reveals what is crooked when they are laid alongside each other. There are questions that will throw you for a loop, but you can always reach for sound doctrine! When you are asked a question, lay it alongside the Word of God, and you will have the straight answer straight-away. Shod your feet with the preparation of the gospel of peace, and you'll be able to practice what you preach.

NINE

Faithful

Above All

Above all, taking the shield of faith with which you will be able to quench all the fiery darts of the wicked one. And take the helmet of salvation, and the sword of the Spirit, which is the word of God.

Ephesians 6:16–17

This "above all" admonition should make us pause. *Above all!* Paul is telling us that *this* is the most important weapon. *Take* the shield of faith. Don't leave it. Take hold of it. Take it in hand and lift it up. *Shield* yourself with faith. You need it because it will quench *all* the fiery darts of the wicked one—every one of them. The arrows will come, but we will remain intact.

If someone fires the flaming arrow of perceived biblical error and I don't have an immediate answer, my trust is in

God. No need to panic. When I suffer, there is no need to panic. I trust that God still loves me. He is still on the throne, and my salvation is still secure. How do I know this? I believe the promises of God. That's my impenetrable shield. My shield guards me from the fiery darts of fear and doubt.

The helmet goes hand in hand with the shield. My helmet of salvation is in place. I have taken it and put it on. It protects my head from doubt. I *know* in whom I have believed.

If I'm about to approach a stranger or open-air preach and fear and fury come at me like arrows, I don't panic. I quench their fire by not thinking of myself but of the unsaved and their terrible fate. How do I know they are in eternal danger? I *believe* the Scriptures. I believe; therefore, I speak—without letting fear paralyze me.

My faith rests in God alone. "In God we trust. All others pay cash" isn't just a famous witticism, it's biblical. It could save all of us a lot of pain. The Bible tells us it's not wise to trust humankind (see Ps. 118:8; John 2:24–25). We are both sinful and fallible. However, sometimes we don't have much choice. We *have* to trust pilots, surgeons, doctors, dentists, and politicians. We trust planes, chairs, car brakes, and of course elevators. Our hope is that elevators, at the least, would be inspected regularly and subject to strict regulations, but consider the incident that occurred in November 2018:

> It took nearly three hours to rescue six people stuck in an elevator in Chicago's fourth-tallest skyscraper—the 875 North Michigan Avenue building, formerly called the John Hancock Center. CBS Chicago reported that a broken hoist

rope caused the express elevator to malfunction Friday while guests who had just left the Signature Room on the 95th floor rode down toward the lobby.

"At the beginning I believed we were going to die. . . . We were going down and then I felt that we were falling down and then I heard a noise—clack clack clack clack clack clack." . . . They found out later that they had careened from the 95th floor down to the 11th floor.[1]

The City of Chicago requires annual inspections of all of its twenty-two thousand elevators. The elevator that failed that morning passed its most recent inspection, which was just a few months before the incident. Even our best human efforts to be trustworthy can fail. Is your faith in human hands or in the hands of God?

The Sword

Putting on the armor of God shows our trust in God. We are of course to *take hold* of the sword of the Spirit, which is the Word of God: "For the word of God is living and powerful, and sharper than any two-edged sword, piercing even to the division of soul and spirit, and of joints and marrow, and is a discerner of the thoughts and intents of the heart" (Heb. 4:12).

Here again are the wonderful words of Spurgeon, known as the Prince of Preachers:

The Word of God is that by which sin is slain, and grace is born in the heart. It is the light which brings life with it. How active and energetic it is, when the soul is convicted of sin, in bringing it forth into gospel liberty! We have seen men shut up as in the devil's own dungeon, and we have tried to get them free. We have shaken the bars of iron, but we could not tear them out so as to set the captives at liberty. But the Word of the Lord is a great breaker of bolts and bars. It not only casts down the strongholds of doubt, but it cuts off the head of Giant Despair. No cell or cellar in Doubting Castle can hold a soul in bondage when the Word of God, which is the master key, is once put to its true use, and made to throw back bolts of despondency. It is living and energetic for encouragement and enlargement. O beloved, what a wonderful power the gospel has to bring us comfort! It brought us to Christ at first, and it still leads us to look to Christ till we grow like Him.[2]

The Sharp Knife

But what if using our sword leads to pain—for us or for the people we evangelize? Good. Pain and discomfort often lead to action. For many years, I had a common spinal condition known as spondylolisthesis. Over three million Americans suffer from it. My pain was the worst first thing in the morning, so I concluded it was caused by pressure on my spine as I lay on my back in bed. So I got a sharp knife and cut a ten-inch-diameter and six-inch-deep mini Grand Canyon into the mattress. That fixed the pain immediately. It was so much better that I became overconfident and about a month later carried part of a lazy boy recliner from Sue's car into our living room. It was a dumb thing to do. The pain came back. That is, until I had another idea. I put a T-shirt on backward and slipped a tennis ball into the pocket on the back. I couldn't sleep on my back. That fixed the pain, and I leaped out of bed each morning with great joy.

The pain led to action. It's the same principle as putting a stone in somebody's shoe. Greg Koukl said of his evangelistic practice:

> Here is my own more modest goal. I want to put a stone in [a nonbeliever's] shoe. All I want to do is give him something worth thinking about. I want him to hobble away on a nugget of truth that annoys him in a good way, something he can't simply ignore because it continues to poke at him.[3]

We bring people the law, because that's what the law does—it puts a stone in their shoes, some pain in their backs. Something has to change. The Commandments stir up guilt and remove false peace that all is well between God and them. It's painful, but it's necessary pain in order to bring them to the cross. Their alternative is hell, so don't pull any punches in your pleading. Better a hand be cut off and an eye plucked out than for them to die in their sins (see Matt. 5:29–30).

Reluctant Bobby

It's not easy to get people to come on camera to be interviewed for YouTube or for our television show. Every now and then, someone will say "Sure" without even knowing what I'm going to ask. But most begin by declining. That's when I go through a routine. I ask if they're shy and tell them I will help them relax on camera. I promise that if they don't like the interview, I'll end it immediately. Then I offer gift cards. I ask for their name and tell them that my questions are about the afterlife. If they respond with something interesting, I tell them how great that would be on camera. Sometimes, people change their minds and say, "I'll do it!" and I respond with, "Thanks for being a good sport," and ask what they do for a living. I keep in mind that my battle isn't against flesh and blood; the enemy knows that a good interview will get hundreds of thousands if not millions of views on our YouTube channel.

I can tell if someone has good interview potential in about ten seconds. Such was the case with a man named Bobby. He was confident and had a great personality, but for some reason he didn't want to come on camera. He just said, "I don't do social media." He had gold in his front tooth, and he had a really nice smile. It was golden. I went through the usual routine I do with decliners, but he wouldn't budge. So I did what I normally do when that happens: share the gospel anyway.

He thought he was a good person, but when I took him through the Ten Commandments, he said he had lied and stolen but hadn't blasphemed God's name. Then a sword fight began.

He said he'd never committed adultery. I told him that Jesus said if we lust after a woman we commit adultery in our hearts. Bobby said that Jesus didn't say that. I said that Jesus did in Matthew 5:28. If that was true, Bobby said, then God hasn't given us free will—"Show me any man who claims he has never lusted after a woman, and I will show you a liar." I said there were gay men who never lusted after women. He laughed and conceded the point but went back to saying that we didn't have a free will and couldn't be held responsible for lusting after women. I told him to try that in a court of law. "Tell the judge that you couldn't help raping a woman because you didn't have a free will. He will throw the book at you because you are morally responsible."

I was right in my conviction that Bobby would have been great on camera. When I shared the gospel, he listened intently. Then he confided that he was once a Christian. I told him that more than likely he had a false conversion and gave him a gift card and one of our movie cards, and we parted congenially. Not all sword fights have to end badly, but the important thing to remember is that you need to be armed to fight!

A Small Puddle

We must remember to use our swords and our faithful words in a manner that is careful and precise. Disaster can happen when we don't! I couldn't help but think of a proverb when one day I noticed a small puddle of water outside of our shower. I believed that the leak was coming from inside the shower basin, so I caulked the inside. But a puddle still appeared after using the shower. My plumber diagnosed the problem, saying there was a leak above the showerhead. Water leaked down the wall between the bathroom and our bedroom and seeped into the carpet, causing a lot of water damage and the beginning of mold. Here's that proverb:

> The beginning of strife is like releasing water;
> Therefore stop contention before a quarrel starts.
> (Prov. 17:14)

Be aware of this in your evangelism. If strife starts, stop the contention before it becomes catastrophic. Clear up misunderstandings. Don't accuse anyone of anything. Be a peacemaker. Be quick to apologize. The Scriptures warn that if we guard our tongues, we will save ourselves a lot of pain:

> Whoever guards his mouth and tongue
> Keeps his soul from troubles. (Prov. 21:23)

But contention is everywhere! Our world thrives on it. It's the basis of a good movie script, book, or documentary. It is the lifeblood of entertainment. If you can show a husband and wife disagreeing on some important issue, business partners clashing like two rams in mating season, or evil pit against good, you have the world's attention. This is especially true with scandal. That has instant tension and is gold to a reporter.

Let's say someone leaks a story that a respected politician, with five kids and a happy marriage, was seen with a woman of disrepute. The press leaks it to the public. Suddenly other women come out of the closet and accuse the politician of multiple improprieties, and it becomes a flood of headlines around the world. Headlines mean sales and more advertisers, and that means more money. The media is like hungry vultures, feeding on the dying flesh of the politician's family. Pictures of a crying wife, distressed kids, rumors of a divorce, and statements from neighbors, old friends, lawyers, or prostitutes are all legitimate fodder. Anything is reportable, no matter how unverified.

The media justifies the slander, saying that the politician is a hypocrite and deserves to suffer. Those who cover the story seem to forget that they are not without sin, and so they don't hesitate to cast the first stone. They take the moral high ground without mercy because they think they are safe from the flood of their own moral indiscretions. But they're not. They too have a multitude of sins, most of which they think are secret. But there's no such thing. The Bible warns:

> You, therefore, have no excuse, you who pass judgment on someone else, for at whatever point you judge another, you are condemning yourself, because you who pass judgment do the same things. Now we know that God's judgment against those who do such things is based on truth. So when you, a mere human being, pass judgment on them and yet do the same things, do you think you will escape God's judgment? (Rom. 2:1–3)

The world doesn't realize that their sins have been leaked to high Heaven. There is big contention between good and evil. The headlines are laid out and ready for publication on judgment day: "For nothing is secret that will not be revealed, nor anything hidden that will not be known and come to light" (Luke 8:17).

Every shameful deed, every idle word, and every sinful thought will be published and will be evidence of our shame and guilt—unless our sins have been washed away by the precious blood of the Lamb. The law gives sinners a glimpse of that day while divine mercy is still being offered. So take up your sword and your shield. Get ready to fight—but don't fight like the world fights with strife and contention. Fight, but fight faithfully.

TEN

Prayerful

Being Frank

[Pray] always with all [kinds of] prayer and supplication in the Spirit, being watchful to this end with all perseverance and supplication for all the saints—and for me, that utterance may be given to me, that I may open my mouth boldly to make known the mystery of the gospel, for which I am an ambassador in chains; that in it I may speak boldly, as I ought to speak.

Ephesians 6:18–20

All of us need to pray, and all of us need to be prayed for—all of the time with all perseverance. Prayer is like oxygen. It is essential for the health of our lives in Christ. If we want to be effective in reaching out, we must be effectual in reaching up. Light always needs a power source. Our source is God: "God is light, and in Him is no darkness at all" (1 John 1:5).

143

We must pray because we have a deadly enemy. Look at this question posed in the comments section of our YouTube channel:

> Hi Ray, I have been struggling lately. Umm . . . I'm gay . . . but not living an actively gay lifestyle, and I'm sort of in this limbo stage between right and left . . . and I don't know what to do. I feel like God wants me to shout, "I'm gay!" or He wants me to knock over a glass of water, and that will get me right with God. . . . Are these just intrusive thoughts, from demons telling me to do these radical things? Sorry if this doesn't make any sense. I just wanted to get your opinion on these thoughts. Are they commands from God? Have you ever done anything radical or embarrassing for God like the things just mentioned? Please let me know what you think. James

What James said makes perfect sense. The carnal mind is an open door for the father of lies. John MacArthur says:

> Do I need to remind you that all false religion and all idols propagate demon doctrine and are energized by seducing demon spirits? False religion is the playground of demons. Second Corinthians tells us in chapter 11 that Satan and his angels disguise themselves as angels of light and become the purveyors of religion. They call men to worship here or there, this system or that system, this idol or that idol, but behind the system and behind the idol are demons. Idols are more than just carved images, false religions are more than just systems of belief. They are demon-energized from the very start.[1]

James is confused because he thinks that the voices in his mind might be from God, and that is the devil's diabolical deception. Our wrestle is against the demonic world, while the unsaved *are held captive* by the enemy. Our hope is that "they may come to their senses and escape the snare of the devil, having been taken captive by him to do his will" (2 Tim. 2:26). His will is adultery, fornication, uncleanness, lewdness, idolatry, sorcery, hatred, contentions, jealousies, outbursts of wrath, selfish ambitions, dissensions, heresies, envy, murders, drunkenness, and revelries (see Gal. 5:20–21). Add to that list confusion and suicide.

That's the frightening battle in which James finds himself. He doesn't have a shield of faith for protection from the fiery darts of the wicked one. He is thrown into confusion because he is not praying with all prayer and supplication. He doesn't *believe* that Satan is walking about as a roaring lion, seeking whom he may devour. If James was a *believer*, he would know that unwanted thoughts that invade his mind are demonic.

But the believer resists the fiery darts of lust, sexual uncleanliness, murder, suicide, envy, and hatred. The difference is that we know the source of these evils, and we are equipped to resist them. The deeper we get into the battle, the more intense the attacks will become. If we don't stay busy in battle, and instead like David walk the rooftops of our imagination, the devil will have a Bathsheba bathing before our eyes. And we know where that leads.

Divine Priority

One sure way to have people speak well of you is to die. Our culture doesn't like to speak evil of the dead. It's disrespectful.

However, Jesus didn't seem to be a big funeral fan. He ruined them. He stopped funeral marches and raised the dead. He spoke Lazarus's name loud enough to raise the dead. His words burst like beams of bright morning light into the dark tomb. Look at where He put funerals on His priority list:

Then He said to another, "Follow Me."
But he said, "Lord, let me first go and bury my father."
Jesus said to him, "Let the dead bury their own dead, but you go and preach the kingdom of God." (Luke 9:59–60)

He wasn't being insensitive to grieving relatives or being disrespectful of the dead. Rather, He was reminding us of our priorities. Eulogizing the dead may be wonderfully consoling to loved ones, but it doesn't save a soul. The gospel does that. *It* is the power of God unto salvation, and if guilty sinners don't hear it, they cannot be saved. They will justly go to hell. I rarely think of this happening without having my breath pulled from my lungs and tears come to my eyes. I hope you feel the same and that you prioritize your time to plead with the living before the grim reaper cuts them down like ripe and ready wheat.

Filmmaker Alfred Hitchcock balked at the idea of having music in the 1944 film *Lifeboat* because he thought the audience wouldn't know where the music was coming from. The musical arranger retorted, "Ask Hitch where the cameras are coming from."[2]

Movies showcase the power of our imaginations. Even though we know that a story line isn't true and that people are merely acting, we can get so caught up in it that we weep at what we see and hear. Yet it's nothing more than make-believe. We weep as we watch a fictitious movie about a dog dying or a prize horse having to be shot, but we are dry-eyed when we *know* sinners are going to hell. We believe the make-believe of Hollywood, but we don't believe the reality of the testimony of Jesus Christ. How can we increase our faith? The short answer is prayer. Again, it's the groaning we spoke of earlier that comes because we believe Scripture and that manifests itself in all kinds of "prayer and supplication in the Spirit."

The Fear of Failure

Back in October 2018, astronaut Nick Hague was supposed to travel to the International Space Station for a six-month stay. Instead, he and his fellow astronaut came tumbling back to Earth after a booster failure a few minutes into the launch. Hague said:

> I imagined that my first trip to outer space was going to be a memorable one. . . . I didn't expect it to be quite this memorable. . . . It went from normal to something-was-wrong pretty quick. It was one bumpy roller-coaster ride, a lot of side-to-side motion, being tossed around, but it was over almost before it started. . . . I knew once I saw that light that we had an emergency with the booster, that at that point we weren't going to make it to orbit that day—so the mission changed to getting back down on the ground as safely as we could.

The astronauts were well-prepared for failure. Hague added, "This is not the first in-flight emergency that I've been a part of. . . . I've spent the better part of the last two years in Star City, Russia, inside a descent module where they have thrown every failure imaginable at us. . . . We had actually run some scenarios where we had a booster failure and [they tested] our response to that."[3]

Here's the difference between the Christian and those astronauts. Although we may prepare for plan B, for us there is no such thing as a failure. When Stephen was being stoned to death for his preaching, it was not a failure. He knew that God was allowing it for His eternal purposes. Jesus was watching from His throne. Nothing is hidden from His eyes, not even the future. He saw the hate-filled Saul of Tarsus who was there that day as the apostle of love. God turns ashes into beauty. Therefore, no matter what comes our way, we must be "steadfast, immovable, *always abounding in the work of the Lord, knowing that your labor is not in vain in the Lord*" (1 Cor. 15:58, emphasis added).

The Shadow

Part of being well-prepared is having answers to questions and objections that may arise from the world's misunderstandings. Keep in mind that our goal isn't to win an argument but to gently guide the hopeless and helpless to safety. The Bible pictures death as a great shadow cast by the moral law. It hangs over sinners like a black and fearful storm and thunders, "The soul that sins shall die. The wages of sin is death." The Bible says that humanity is *sitting* in the valley of the shadow of death (see Luke 1:79). Every time they sin, they store up wrath. If Satan fell like lightning for the sin of pride, how much more will wrath fall upon those who have a *multitude* of sins, whose hearts are deceitfully wicked, who drink iniquity like water, and who love darkness and hate the light?

Yet there is a rock in the valley of the shadow of death on which light shines through the dark clouds. On this rock, mercy rejoices over judgment. Those who come to the rock of God's mercy are no longer under the shadow of His wrath. The darkness cannot overcome the light. Life conquered death!

This reality should make us run toward unbelievers, eager for them to share in our victory. But in our ignorant zeal, we can sometimes cause damage to the gospel. We must remember that without God's help, we can do nothing. All of our pleadings are nothing but dead words if the Holy Spirit doesn't bring them to life. So we must do everything in prayer. We pray before we present the gospel, we are prayerful while we speak, and we pray after we conclude, because we know that salvation is of the Lord. Every time we open our mouths for the kingdom of God, we are exercising trust—faith that God will take our words and drive them home to the sinner's conscience. Again, if that doesn't happen, nothing happens. We have merely had a conversation with someone about Heaven and hell.

Without constant prayer and openness to correction from God, we make grievous mistakes in our evangelism. One common mistake is telling unbelievers they will end up in hell *because they reject Jesus.* That is said to be the ultimate sin. Let's play this scenario out.

Say you have discovered a tribe in Africa that has never had contact with the outside world, let alone heard the gospel.

As you peer through the bushes, you realize that because they've never been contacted, they've *never* heard of Jesus. If sin is rejecting Jesus, this tribe hasn't sinned because they've never even heard His name. How can you reject someone about whom you've never heard?

Here now is your dilemma. At the moment, they haven't sinned because sin is rejecting Jesus. But if you preach Jesus to them, *and they reject Him,* they will go to hell—*and you will be the one who sent them there.* Therefore, it would be kind of you to keep your mouth shut and not tell them about Jesus. In the light of the Great Commission of Mark 16:15 to preach the gospel to every creature, such a scenario is ludicrous.

Rejecting Jesus is not the ultimate sin. This terrible error is often based on a misunderstanding of the words of Jesus: "And when He has come, He will convict the world of sin, and of righteousness, and of judgment: of sin, because they do not believe in Me; of righteousness, because I go to My Father and you see Me no more; of judgment, because the ruler of this world is judged" (John 16:8–11).

Let's look at these verses in the bigger context. The Holy Spirit convicts the world of sin. *We* don't do that. And we don't do it because we can't. We can only show sinners the gravity of their sins. We are to simply preach the gospel. We do what Jesus did and precede the gospel with the law (see Mark 10:17–19). In doing so, we work in concert with the Holy Spirit, who convicts the world of sin (which is trans-gression of the law; see 1 John 3:4), of righteousness (which is of the law), and of judgment (which is by the law; see Rom. 2:12; James 2:12).

Jesus said in John 16:9 that the Holy Spirit would convict the world "*of sin,* because they do not believe in Me" (emphasis added). They won't be sent to hell for rejecting Jesus. They'll be sent to hell for embracing their sins! If they reject Him *and die in their sins,* they will be judged for lying, stealing, adultery, fornication, blasphemy, and every other manner of sin. We must do what Jesus did if we want them to see their need of the Savior. Jesus spoke of sinners dying in their sins *twice* in one verse: "Therefore I said to you that *you will die in your sins;* for if you do not believe that I am He, *you will die in your sins*" (John 8:24, emphasis added).

Judgment will come *because* sinners die in their sins.

John 3:18 is another verse often used out of context to tell sinners they will go to hell for rejecting Jesus: "He who believes in Him is not condemned; but he who does not believe is condemned already, because he has not believed in the name of the only begotten Son of God." But immediately following this verse, Jesus tells us *why* sinners are "condemned already": "And this is the condemnation, that the light has come into the world, and men loved darkness rather than light, *because their deeds were evil*" (v. 19, emphasis added).

Sinners are condemned because their *deeds* are evil. They are condemned because they transgressed the moral law, for "sin is transgression of the law" (1 John 3:4).

Instead of telling unbelievers they will go to hell for rejecting Jesus, we must give them the law to show them they have sinned against God, and pray that the Holy Spirit convicts them of their sin. Once they realize that their sins have offended God, you present the gospel. You preach Jesus to them—the one who was crucified for the sin of the world. If they then fail to believe in Jesus *and die in their sins*, they will be judged for their sins—not for their unbelief. The terrible consequence of dying without the Savior will be the wrath of the law.

We *reason* with sinners because we want them to understand that the claims of the gospel are *reasonable*. To tell them that they're going to hell for not believing in Jesus is unreasonable. It doesn't make sense, it's not biblical, and it hardens hearts.

Paul's Example

We should reason with sinners about sin, righteousness, and judgment to come. We have the example in Scripture of what Paul did with Felix: "After some days, when Felix came with his wife Drusilla, who was Jewish, he sent for Paul and heard him concerning the faith in Christ. Now as he reasoned about righteousness, self-control, and the judgment to come, Felix was afraid and answered, 'Go away for now; when I have a convenient time I will call for you'" (Acts 24:24–25).

We read that Paul presented "the faith in Christ" to Felix and his wife by reasoning with them about righteousness, self-control (the sin of the governor was obviously intemperance), and judgment to come. Paul worked with the Holy Spirit who (again) convicts the world of sin, and of righteousness, and of judgment. Clearly, Felix wasn't fearful because of the good news of the gospel. Good news doesn't have that effect. Rather, he trembled because he realized he had sinned by transgressing the law and came under conviction.

The law still has that terrifying effect, but people in our age have become numb to it. Bible teacher Paris Reidhead says:

> If I had my way, I would declare a moratorium on public preaching of "the plan of salvation" in America for one to two years. Then I would call on everyone who has use of the airways and the pulpits to preach the holiness of God, the righteousness of God and the Law of God, until sinners would cry out, "What must we do to be saved?" Then I would take them off in a corner and whisper the gospel to them. Such drastic action is needed because we have gospel-hardened a generation of sinners by telling them how to be saved before they have any understanding why they need to be saved.[4]

If we want sinners to tremble and come to Christ for mercy, we must do what Paul did. We must understand the function of God's law, which is to bring the knowledge of sin and to show how "exceedingly sinful" sin is (see Rom. 3:19, 20; 7:13). If God is as holy as the law reveals Him to be, hell is *reasonable*—and that is what makes the gospel understandable.

An Eighty-Six-Year-Old Atheist Scientist

But a reasonable, prayerful presentation of the gospel still comes head-to-head with the unreasonable nature of human beings. Let me tell you about another one of my encounters in evangelism. As I rode my bike through the park, I saw an elderly man hobbling slowly toward his car. Normally, I avoid asking elderly people to come on camera because they typically don't want to, but for some reason I rode right up to this gentleman and asked if he would like to be on YouTube.

He didn't want to do it, but I persisted by saying that I wanted to ask him about the afterlife. That stirred something in him. He said he was a scientist, was raised a Catholic, and didn't believe that God existed or that there was an afterlife. That sent me into my pleading mode. I told him that he would be a wonderful interviewee, that I wanted to speak to people like him, that our YouTube channel had millions of views, and that I would give him a Subway gift card. He wouldn't budge, so I changed the subject.

I looked at Sam and asked the man, "Do you like dogs?" He thought they were wonderful, so I said, "Let's talk about dogs." That did it. A few minutes later, I was set up and we began the interview.[5] He told me his name was Frank. Once he seemed relaxed being on camera, I commented, "Frank, you said that you were a scientist." He began talking about the magnificence of the heavens and how he had liked to gaze at the stars as a young boy. Then he said, "I'd look up at the stars and I'd think [blasphemy] how beautiful the universe is."

I then asked if he used to pray when he did that because I had just heard him use the name of God when he talked about looking up at the stars.

"I don't use his name in vain: it's an expression with me. I rarely say that. It was an accident." Then he closed his eyes and reverentially said, "I think of the Mighty One, which refers to the sun. The sun is the Mighty One. What a beautiful thing."

I asked, "Who made it?"

"Who made it? We don't know."

I said, "*You* don't know."

Frank said that I didn't know. I said that I did, and when he asked "Who?" I told him that God created the sun. At this, he laughed. I told him that the sun is ninety-three-million miles away, and yet it's just warm enough to ripen our tomatoes. Did he think it was a coincidence or was there design behind it? He responded, "I'm amazed at how orderly it is. But I can counter anything you say. I'm the guy who loves to base my beliefs on facts. And you don't have the facts! You have false beliefs because you read the Bible. That's fine, it's a great book."

He then began to judge God for His supposed inaction. God judged Sodom and Gomorrah, but He didn't bother judging the world today. We're just as evil. This was one of the reasons Frank didn't believe in God's existence. He believed the insanity that nothing created everything because God allowed evil to exist.

It was time to bring out the cannons. We'd had our intellectual sword fight. It could have gone on all day—Frank didn't want to surrender. He could outwit me and had a thousand other reasons to reject what I was saying. So I swung to the conscience. I asked, "Do you think you're a good person?" He said yes.

It never ceases to amaze and encourage me that the Scriptures are so right when it comes to humanity. Proverbs 20:6

says, "Most [people] will proclaim each [their] own good-ness." Notice it says "most." I would estimate that it's about 90 percent. We think we are good because we judge by our own low moral standard, and from there we consider our-selves right with God. This error is rooted in the idolatrous thought that God is just like us. Fortunately, we have His law to correct this error and dash sinners' false hopes that they are heading for Heaven when in reality they are heading for hell.

Frank was a professing atheist, but we (as Christians) have inside information on the unsaved through the Scriptures. *Every* sinner believes in the existence of God. He has given light to *everyone* via the conscience, and the heavens (in-cluding the mighty sun) declare His glory. Atheism is willful ignorance of that light. It is a denial of that which is intui-tive. I knew that when I took Frank through the moral law, his conscience would bear witness (see Rom. 2:15). If he was humble, he would agree with the moral law and see his dan-ger, and then the gospel would be good news of God's mercy. If he was proud, the gospel would remain foolishness to him.

"How many lies have you told in your lifetime?"

Frank cussed and asked, "Who can count?"

I told him that God could. In fact, He knew every word before it was even on his tongue (see Ps. 139:4).

Frank laughed and said, "Your belief is that if I live a good life and do all the things that He professes, I will go to Heaven. Hallelujah."

I told him that he had it wrong. He asked, "How do you get into Heaven?"

"Let me tell you. Have you ever stolen anything, even if small?" Frank said he had. He had also used God's name in vain, claiming, "I do, but not on purpose." When I asked if he had ever looked at a woman with lust, he smiled and said, "Of course. I'm only human. Who lives a perfect life?"

He continued to laugh, even when I said I wasn't judging him but that he had just told me that he was a lying, thieving, blasphemous adulterer at heart. But his demeanor changed when I asked if he would be innocent or guilty on judgment day.

It's been rightly said that law without consequence is nothing but good advice. The Ten Commandments are a great way to live. No stealing, adultery, or murder. That would be a happy society. But if God holds us morally accountable and threatens punishment for transgression of the law, proud hearts get offended.

Frank admitted that he would be guilty on judgment day. When I asked "Heaven or hell?" he became angry, cussed, and said there was no such place.

As I explained the cross, Frank rolled his eyes in mocking contempt. He ignored the gospel and said, "No one can uphold all those laws. We're human beings! We live together; we're going to make mistakes."

I tried again by saying we had broken God's law. Frank stopped me and said he hadn't broken any laws because he didn't believe in them—as if ignorance of the law will be an excuse on judgment day. But we are not ignorant. Because of the testimony of our consciences, we are without excuse.

I knew that the only way I would be able to share the gospel without him angrily butting in was to personalize it. And that's what I did. I told him that I had lied, lusted, broken the commandments, and was heading for hell. "But the Bible says that even though we broke God's Law, He is rich in mercy." Again, Frank rolled his eyes in mocking contempt. The gospel rolled off him like water off a duck's back. It was foolishness to him because he refused to humble himself and acknowledge that he had sinned against God.

Remember that the apostle Paul asked for prayer that he would be able to speak boldly and make known "the mystery of the gospel." The gospel is a mystery in one way in that it makes no sense to the proud. It is even foolishness to them: "For the message of the cross is foolishness to those who are perishing, but to us who are being saved it is the power of God" (1 Cor. 1:18).

The good news of someone paying a fine for me will seem foolish, ridiculous, and mysterious if I refuse to acknowledge that I have broken any laws. That's why every mention of the cross to Frank was met with hardhearted mockery, sarcasm, and proud cynicism.

Read Spurgeon's exposition on pride:

Pride, to begin with, I am afraid, may be set down as *the sin of human nature*. If there is a sin that is universal, it is this. Where is it not to be found? Hunt among the highest and loftiest in the world, and you shall find it there; and then go and search among the poorest and the most miserable, and you shall find it there. There may be as much pride inside a beggar's rags as in a prince's robe; and a harlot may be as proud as a model of chastity. Pride is a strange creature; it never objects to its lodgings. It will live comfortably enough in a palace, and it will live equally at its ease in a hovel. Is there any man in whose heart pride does not lurk? If anyone held up his hand, and said, "I am one," I would answer,

"That is Number One in the widest street of the whole city of Self-conceit"; for, when we fancy that we have clean escaped from pride, it is only because we have lost the sense of its weight through being surrounded with it. A man who bears a bowl of water feels its weight, but if he goes right into the water, it will be all over him, and yet he will not notice the burden of it. He who lives in pride up to the neck—no, he who is over head and heels in pride, is the most likely to imagine that he is not proud at all.[6]

Some may have given up on Frank because of what Jesus says: "Do not give what is holy to the dogs; nor cast your pearls before swine, lest they trample them under their feet, and turn and tear you in pieces" (Matt. 7:6).

But does the command not to "cast your pearls before swine" really mean that we are to give up on a proud person and move on? If someone doesn't embrace the gospel and thinks it is nothing but foolishness, isn't this casting pearls before swine? If you throw a pearl to a pig, it won't even sniff it. It has no value to a pig. And our most precious pearl— Christ on the cross—has no value to proud sinners. Why? Because they don't truly see their own sins as being serious.

Should I therefore give up on Frank and move on to someone who will appreciate the pearl of the gospel? No, definitely not. Instead, look again at *why* he doesn't value the gospel. It's because he doesn't see his sin and therefore his consequent and terrible danger.

Of course, we shouldn't give the pearl of the gospel to those who don't give it any value. They don't need the gospel yet; they first need the law to reveal what's missing—the knowledge of sin. We need to remember what Paul said, "I would not have known sin except through the law" (Rom. 7:7).

There was a time when our own understanding was also darkened, and we were alienated from the life of God through the ignorance that was in us because of the blindness in our hearts (see Eph. 4:18). We loved the darkness and hated the light; neither would we come to the light because our deeds would be exposed. Had someone given us the gospel, we would have given no value to it while we were in that state. We needed the law to show us that we needed mercy. This is why Sinai should always precede Calvary.

Jesus said in Mark 16:15 to "go into all the world and preach the gospel to every creature." That is our mandate. When we have hard soil, we should break it up with the plow of God's law as Jesus did (see Mark 10:17–19). Once the ground is soft, then it's ready for the seed. Don't give up on anyone while they are listening. Just keep going back to the law and breaking up the hard soil. Jesus did this often with hypocritical religious leaders. He rebuked them and spoke of judgment because He loved them. We should do the same.

See Spurgeon again as he speaks of the function of the law:

A man who says, "I have kept the law," does not know what the law means. Perhaps he supposes that those ten great commandments only refuse him certain outward things; but he does not know that they are all spiritual—that, for instance, if the commandment says, "You shall not commit adultery," it is not merely the act of adultery that is forbidden, but every sin of the kind—every tendency to lewdness—every unchaste word or thought, for so Christ explains it: "I say unto you, that whosoever looks on a woman to lust after her has committed adultery with her already in his heart." This makes the law look very different from the mere casual reading of it that many give. If it says, "You shall not covet," any thought of a desire to gain that which is my neighbor's, by unlawful means, in discontent with God's providence, comes under that law. So is it with all the commands; they are spiritual, they are far-reaching, and when a man understands their true character, he cries, "O my God, I have indeed broken Your holy law; how could I have kept it? From the first moment when I sinned, my fallen nature has incapacitated me from ever keeping this thrice-holy law of Yours."[7]

It was Frank's mockery that told me I had to go back to the law. Those who don't have the moral law as part of their essential weaponry naturally give up on hard-hearted sinners. But those of us who have seen the power of the law to bring the knowledge of sin, and thus pave the way for the gospel, never give up. How could we, if we love sinners?

Frank needed to understand that he was a sinner who was in great danger so that the gospel would make sense. I went back to reasoning with him about his sins and his responsibility to a holy God. I told him that I loved him and that was why I was talking to him. I then made him laugh by saying that if I kept speaking to him he was going to have a heart attack, and I didn't want to be responsible for his death.

I turned off the camera, and Frank and I talked for another fifteen minutes or so before parting as though we were old friends. He may have been able to argue with the message but not the love.

Never give up on a soul. No one is a hopeless case as long as there is air in their lungs. If you are thinking of someone who is hard-hearted, and you've written him off as a lost cause, answer me this: Has that person stood by while others murder Christians? Has he held their clothes while they kill them? Is he breathing out threats and slaughter against the church, going from house to house and arresting them, torturing them, and putting them to death (see Acts 8:3)? Is he a blasphemer, a persecutor, and an insolent man (see 1 Tim. 1:13)? If anyone fits the description of a hardheaded, hard-nosed, proud person, it was the murderous Saul of Tarsus. But Jesus didn't give up on him—not for a moment. Love doesn't do that.

What Can You Do?

Perhaps as you read John Wesley's words earlier about sleep, your heart sank because you love sleep and appreciate the fact that you can occasionally sleep in. I do too, and I often watch an old movie, or golf, or fall asleep during the day. So relax. There's nothing wrong with that. Maybe you're thinking that if you got up early, it would make the day unbearably long. I know how you feel. If I can't fill in my day with interesting activities, time tends to drag. And that's no fun. But we are promised an abundant life (see John 10:10), and God will honor you if you honor Him.

John Wesley lived centuries before the invention of our modern conveniences, and because of that, his life was no doubt filled with activities about which we know nothing. We have microwaves, heaters, cars, planes, email, iPhones, and many other wonderful conveniences that save us time, which means we have more time on our hands. That is a blessing, not a curse. Use your time to increase your knowledge of God and to reach the lost.

Ralph Barton was an American artist best known for his cartoons and caricatures of actors and other celebrities. He committed suicide on May 19, 1931, and following is part of the tragic note he left behind:

> No one thing is responsible for this and no one person— except myself. If the gossips insist on something more defi- nite and thrilling as a reason, let them choose my pending appointment with the dentist or the fact that I happened to be painfully short of cash at the moment. . . . After all, one has to choose a moment; and the air is always full of reasons at any given moment. I did it because I am fed up with inventing devices for getting through twenty-four hours a day and with bridging over a few months periodically with some beautiful interest, such as a new gal who annoyed me to the point where I forgot my own troubles.[8]

He said, "I did it because I am fed up with inventing de- vices for getting through twenty-four hours a day." If life is just about my self-interests, I will be bored in the selfish pursuit of my personal happiness. But I will *always* have something extremely important to do with my time if I am willing to bring the Word of God to sinners. If I live to do the will of God and long to reach the lost, my work will not be fulfilled until the trumpet sounds.

Don't let this world shape you into being ungrateful. You are different from this evil world. Your sins have been forgiven.

You know that God has given you the gift of life and added the unspeakable consolation of immortality. You know that He is the one who has given you eyes to see, ears to hear, taste buds to enjoy good food. Appreciate these things as fully as you can. Count boredom a by-product of ingratitude. Go back to being a wide-eyed child. Think about the birds you see and hear and how amazing they are. Think about puppies, red roses, sunshine, rain, the beauty of clouds, and the blueness of the sky. Then think about the God who created all these things. He is the lover of your soul, and He proved His love for you in that while you were given to sin, Christ died for you.

In light of Christ's infinite gift, refuse to be bored and ungrateful.

Practical Ways to Redeem Time

Find a favorite chair, get a soft blanket, make a cup of tea or coffee, and set aside a daily time to study the Bible. Have a plan to conquer a certain passage of Scripture. Sometimes I will spend weeks going through a chapter or a book. I have a friend who reads each book of the Bible seven times, making notes as thoughts come to him. This is what it means to *meditate* on the Word of God. Study Psalm 1 and what it promises you when you meditate on Scripture. Read it seven times. Take notes. Dig into the soil until you find gold nuggets.

John Wesley was adamant about the importance of securing a time early in the morning to wait on the Lord.

If you desire to rise early, sleep early; secure this point at all events. In spite of the most dear and agreeable companions, in spite of their most earnest solicitations, in spite of entreaties, railleries, or reproaches, rigorously keep your hour. Rise up precisely at your time, and retire without ceremony. Keep your hour, notwithstanding the most pressing business: Lay all things by till the morning. Be it ever so great a cross, ever so great self-denial, keep your hour, or all is over.[9]

Biologist Christoph Randler surveyed 367 university students, asking what time of day they were most energetic and how willing and able they were to take action to change a situation to their advantage. He says:

When it comes to business success, morning people hold the important cards. My earlier research showed that they tend to get better grades in school, which get them into better colleges, which then lead to better job opportunities. Morning people also anticipate problems and try to minimize them, my survey showed. They're proactive. A number of studies have linked this trait, proactivity, with better job performance, greater career success, and higher wages.[10]

We have a huge advantage over John Wesley. We have the internet. You can enhance your daily quiet time by instantly finding out what Spurgeon or Wesley or other wonderfully gifted Bible teachers or preachers have said of a particular passage. You can, in a matter of seconds, find atheist sites, log in, and testify for the gospel. I have notes on my iPad that I can cut and paste in the comments sections of videos I find. You can create your own "instant answer," in which you explain why there is suffering, how we can know God exists, and why the Bible is trustworthy and give your own testimony. You could be influential in bringing someone to the Savior simply because each day you spent twenty minutes surfing for sinners, taking to heart that whoever "turns a sinner from the error of [their] way will save a soul from death and cover a multitude of sins" (James 5:20).

If you become addicted to winning souls, you are being wise with your time. The world is filled with brilliant people who are spending their precious lives doing great things that matter only in this life. That means their grand achievements will in time rust, crumble, and turn into the meaningless dust of antiquity. The billionaire is a pauper to be pitied compared to you and the everlasting riches you have in Christ. You have set your eyes on eternity, and when you win souls (with God's help) what you achieve with your time will last into eternity. Consider this great truth and what Spurgeon says about it:

> The fruit of the righteous is a tree of life,
> And he who wins souls is wise. (Prov. 11:30)

If God shall bless us to the winning of souls, our work shall remain when the wood, and hay, and stubble of earth's art and science shall have gone to the dust from which they sprang. In heaven itself, the soul-winner, blessed of God, shall have memorials of his work preserved forever in the galleries of the skies. He has selected a wise object, for what can be wiser than to glorify God, and what, next to that, can be wiser than in the highest sense to bless our fellow men; to snatch a soul from the gulf that yawns, to lift it up to the heaven that glorifies; to deliver an immortal from the thraldom of Satan, and to bring him into the liberty of Christ?[11]

I have spent my life "winning souls." But all I have truly done is plant the seed of the Word of God in the hearts of hell-bound sinners, praying that God will bring it to life. I'm nothing but an unprofitable servant, yet the Bible calls me a soul winner and tells me I'm wise. When I pass from this mortal life, I have the joy of knowing I didn't live to gather riches that someone else will spend, nor for the experience of fleeting fame or the emptiness of the praise of people. I was a lowly servant of the Lord. I had the honor of preaching the glorious gospel. If God saw fit to bless my little labors, then what I put my time into will last. And so will yours, if you so direct your energies toward the lost. Look again at the soul-stirring words of Spurgeon:

> Mark ye well, my brethren, that he who is successful in soul-winning, will prove to have been a wise man in the judgment of those who see the end as well as the beginning. Even if I were utterly selfish, and had no care for anything but my own happiness, I would choose, if I might, under God, to be a soul-winner, for never did I know perfect, overflowing, unutterable happiness of the purest and most ennobling order, till I first heard of one who had sought and found a Savior through my means. I recollect the thrill of joy which went through me! No young mother ever rejoiced so much over her first-born child—no warrior was so exultant over a hard-won victory. Oh! the joy of knowing that a sinner once at enmity has been reconciled to God by the Holy Spirit, through the words spoken by our feeble lips. Since then, by grace given to me, the thought of which prostrates me in self-abasement, I have seen and heard of, not hundreds only, but even thousands of sinners turned

from the error of their ways by the testimony of God in me. Let afflictions come, let trials be multiplied as God willeth, still this joy preponderates above all others, the joy that we are unto God a sweet savor of Christ in every place, and that as often as we preach the Word, hearts are unlocked, bosoms heave with a new life, eyes weep for sin, and their tears are wiped away as they see the great Substitute for sin, and live. Beyond all controversy it is a joy worth worlds to win souls, and thank God, it is a joy that does not cease with this mortal life.[12]

Many atheists and other unsaved people watch our YouTube channel. They gather like mosquitoes ready to sting. When they leave hateful comments, I respond by saying something like: "Good to have you here. Maybe you could watch *Evolution vs. God* on YouTube. It has millions of views. Love to know what you think about it. Best wishes, Ray Comfort."

A gentle and kind answer is a balm for any stinging comment, and more often than not, I get wonderfully polite replies. You can do the same sort of thing each day by replying to negative comments on our Living Waters YouTube channel or other channels. Just watching the reaction of sinners may stir up your zeal. We get many encouraging comments and emails from those who are catching the disease of evangelism and choosing not to live in the ease of complacency about the lost. Following is another comment:

> Ray, ever since a friend and I started watching your YouTube channel and exploring your website, we began to implement

what we were learning. We also studied Scripture to validate what we learned.

We have a street witnessing ministry called "Not Ashamed." We have seen a dramatic increase in the number of people who engage with us on the street by what you have shared with us.

We also have seen the value of only one person giving the gospel. Whoever engages does the talking. The other one or two listen and pray.

This has taken off so dramatically that our pastor has decided to have us put on an evangelism training using *Way of the Master* and your YouTube videos.

We live in Philadelphia. Others are excited to see engagements in street evangelism on the uptick. The Lord blessing us with some success is working on the hearts of some brothers and sisters who were content to warm a chair in the church.

The congregation and its prayer group are now holding us up and supporting this ministry in prayer. What a blessing.

Keep doing what you do. It makes a difference. Grace and peace, Robert Zanol

If you, like Robert, have found yourself inspired to reach out to the lost, this is what your day could look like: You discipline yourself to rise early. You spend an hour in prayer and study of the Word. You take notes. You spend twenty minutes witnessing to sinners online.

Now it's time to do what you normally do. Go to work or look after your kids at home. On your lunch break, you can again reach into eternity. Do your necessary eating, then go fishing. Find a fishing spot and go there daily. I did that almost every day for twelve years back in New Zealand. When I came to the United States, I had a similar routine. Remember, the fish don't come to you; you have to go to them. Make this a priority in your life. Come rain or shine, go fishing for people.

Whenever I go out on my bike with Sam, I get lots of attention. Maybe you're bored. Maybe you're not retired and not bored. Whether you are young or old, do what I did. Get two pairs of cheap matching sunglasses—one for you and one for your dog. Drill a hole in the side of the glasses. They need to be plastic with a reasonably wide side. Tie some thin elastic through the holes in the glasses so that it goes under the dog's chin and around the back of his neck. Give him a treat every time you put them on. He may shake them off at first, but after awhile he'll equate them with a treat. Sam goes crazy whenever I get ahold of the glasses now because it means something even better than a treat—it means we're going out on the bike.

You don't need to take your dog on a bike. Just take him for a walk where people gather. And arm yourself with our special dog trivia and training tracts.[13] Your pooch will get attention, and that will give you an opportunity to give out the tracts and even share the gospel.

If you have the privilege of being a stay-at-home mom or dad, don't stay at home. Do your fishing at the grocery store or the mall or local university—anywhere people gather. Your aim is to give out a few gospel tracts. Maybe you will give out more. It's up to you, and it will all come down to your attitude. Do you care that human beings are going to hell? Is your concern about possible rejection more important to you than the fact that sinners are going to hell? When a Goliath tries to intimidate you, send a stone into his arrogant forehead by ignoring those fears of rejection.

Final Thoughts

Lingual Frenulum

Below is part of one of the longer YouTube comments among over thirty-three thousand left about our movie *The Atheist Delusion* in which atheists change their minds about the existence of God when confronted with the complexities of DNA. This particular comment is interesting because the writer, unbeknownst to him, reveals his spiritual history.

> The longer I live, the more I become absolutely sure that humans will, and can, believe anything. Anything you can tell them. You create and nurture the fertile ground of human gullibility by quietly ensuring that your average Joe never develops an adequate understanding of what constitutes a sound argument, so that they become susceptible to the influence of totally rubbish arguments. . . . Theological fallacy-laden arguments may seem very compelling, but this is because your ability to counter them has never been adequately developed. . . . Essentially, the longevity of religion's

influence among men is dependent upon society as a whole denying ordinary people the ability to really think/interrogate information. . . . Honestly, ten years ago I could have made a video just like this and I probably would have been pretty chuffed with myself. The reason the man writing this comment could have done that but can't today is because I spent the time trying to make my arguments watertight in order to defeat atheists soundly in debates. In order to do that, I had to learn how to construct a sensible argument. Rather innocently, I discovered that my own stinking pile of arguments, and the stinking selection offered by ironically renowned Christian apologists, would not give me what I need to put atheists in their place. Most cringeworthy of all, everywhere I looked I saw Christians using straw-man fallacies, non sequiturs, the argumentum ad baculum (argument of the stick or cudgel), appeals to authority, bandwagon fallacies, red herrings, ad hominems, and post hoc.

This man, who may have once professed Christianity, is the product of modern evangelistic methods. Rather than the law being used to bring the knowledge of sin, driving him to the cross as his only means of salvation from death and certain judgment, he was "converted" merely through the human intellect. He was intellectually *convinced* of the gospel rather than *converted* by it. He began to sow with the same seed that had caused him to change his mind. He tried to intellectually convince others to come to Christ. His weapons of warfare were carnal, designed to reach the carnal mind, such as straw-man fallacies, non sequiturs, appeals to authority, bandwagon fallacies, and so on. In time, he fell away when other intellectual arguments became more convincing than the one that originally swayed him to embrace the faith.

I'm a Christian because nothing made provision for my sins and impending judgment. Jesus Christ was my sole oasis in the desert. He gave me life when mine was running out. Without Him, I would be under death's power and the just condemnation of the law. I whisper with Peter, "Where shall I go, Lord? You alone have the words of eternal life" (see John 6:68). No religion can forgive sins. But unwavering trust in the integrity of our morally perfect Creator gives me hope.

This commenter was offended not only by God's past judgments but also by eternal judgment. What a fool I would be to turn my back on everlasting life just because I don't understand God's judgments—especially when I'm not meant to understand them:

> How unsearchable are His judgments and His ways past finding out!
>
> "For who has known the mind of the LORD?
> Or who has become His counselor?"
> "Or who has first given to Him
> and it shall be repaid to him?"
>
> For of Him and through Him and to Him are all things, to whom be glory forever. Amen. (Rom. 11:33–36)

The commenter's objection to eternal judgment revealed that he had never seen his own sins as being exceedingly sinful. Nor had he seen the holiness of God. Both of these revelations would have stopped his sinful and proud mouth from standing over almighty God in moral judgment. But they didn't. And so his delusions of moral grandeur hid the cross from him.

This is why any evangelism that leaves out the law in preparing hearts for grace is so dangerous. It merely *convinces* sinners rather than *converts* them. It changes minds, not hearts, and abandons people in the pew who are still in their sin.

In Acts 17:16, Paul was grieving because the whole city of Athens was given to idolatry. They were in violation of the first and second of the Ten Commandments. But he didn't call a prayer meeting for the lost or move on to other priorities. His love caused him to open his mouth and speak. He used the law by preaching against their idolatry and telling them to repent:

> So then, being God's children, we should not think that the Divine Nature (deity) is like gold or silver or stone, an image formed by the art and imagination or skill of man. Therefore God overlooked and disregarded the former ages of ignorance; but now He commands all people everywhere to repent [that is, to change their old way of thinking, to regret their past sins, and to seek God's purpose for their lives], because He has set a day when He will judge the inhabited world in righteousness by a Man whom He has appointed and destined for that task, and He has provided credible proof to everyone by raising Him from the dead. (Acts 17:29–31 AMP)

God overlooked their ignorance. This is because He is rich in mercy, and two thousand years later He is still rich in mercy. So we must *run* to this generation of sinners because the day is quickly coming when the door of His patience will close. On that day, ignorance will not be a defense.

The gospel we preach is *extraordinary* mercy. Humanity doesn't have such mercy for crime:

> Most people are familiar with the legal principle that ignorance of the law is no excuse. This age-old rule prevents individuals from avoiding prosecution by claiming that they did not know their conduct was illegal. In most cases—such as murder, theft, assault, and arson—it is obvious why defendants should not be able to claim ignorance as a defense. But ignorance can, under certain limited circumstances, provide a viable defense to a criminal charge.[1]

Human law has only enough grace for minor lawbreaking. There is nothing amazing about it, and even that door slams shut if ignorance is willful:

> Keep in mind that you cannot purposefully avoid learning applicable criminal laws and then take advantage of your ignorance as a defense. If a prosecutor can demonstrate that you "consciously avoided" knowledge of relevant criminal provisions, a judge at trial would instruct the jury that it should treat you as if you were fully aware of the legal consequences of your conduct. For example, if you opened a restaurant and a health inspector gave you a booklet containing the state's new health laws for food service providers—which you never bothered to read—you would not likely be able to claim ignorance of a criminal provision contained in that booklet during a subsequent prosecution.[2]

The world will be without excuse on judgment day because their ignorance is willful. They have the light of creation and the light of conscience. They also have the light of God's Word. Even if they never bother to read it, they still can't plead ignorance on judgment day, just like the would-be restaurateur who never read the health codes. But our hope is that further light from the law (see Prov. 6:23), the glorious gospel (see 2 Cor. 4:4), and God's love heard in our pleading will cause them to come out of the darkness.

Most cartoons are meant to be funny. However, I saw one cartoon that didn't make me smile. It pictured a doctor with an older man sitting on a table in front of him. The patient's shoulders were drooped, he was struggling to breathe, and the doctor was saying, "Remember the twenty extra years you added to your life through healthy living? Well, this is it."

That one isn't funny because it's tragically true.

If you've made it all the way through this book, and you've not fled to the Savior, let me ask you a question. If you found out that you had a terminal disease, would you search out a cure? No doubt, you would. You would sell everything you owned to obtain a cure to your disease. After all, what's the point in owning anything if you're dead? Nothing compares to the value of your life.

Your prognosis is not good. You are terminal. You are going to die. And so you should put everything on hold until you find a cure for death. Think of Pilgrim in the famous allegory *Pilgrim's Progress*. When he had the revelation that he was terminal, he *ran* out of his home, forsaking his wife and family, crying out, "Life. Life! Eternal life!"[3] Nothing else matters if death takes you. It will rip you from your wife, your family, and all your possessions. So seek after God with all your heart until you find Him because in Him *alone* is eternal life. And *please* do that right now. Don't wait another minute.

Maybe you have already made the decision to follow Christ. Are you inviting anyone else to follow Him with you? Or are you tongue-tied? The best way I have found to "untie" that tongue is through prayer. I once interviewed a Christian lady who told me that she deliberately didn't witness to her unsaved friends. She just "loved on them." When I asked her where they would go if they died in their sins, she hesitated to say they would go to hell. When I asked her if her problem was that she was a little tongue-tied, she said that it was.

We say that someone is tongue-tied when they are shy and don't know what to say. The phrase actually refers to a medical condition describing a shortness of the lingual frenulum—the string or fold under the tongue that allows it movement.

I told this woman about a six-year-old boy in Texas who was tongue-tied. He had a speech impediment that was so bad only his parents could understand what he was saying. They had taken him to speech therapy for five years, and his speech hadn't improved.

However, when a pediatric dentist was checking his teeth, she noticed that the lingual frenulum was short. She stepped out into the waiting room and asked his parents if she could perform a simple and quick operation. They gave their permission, and after a short recovery, the boy was speaking clearly.

We see a similar incident in Scripture. We are told of a man who suffered from a speech impediment:

Then they brought to Him one who was deaf and had an impediment in his speech, and they begged Him to put His hand on him. And He took him aside from the multitude, and put His fingers in his ears, and He spat and touched his tongue. Then, looking up to heaven, He sighed, and said to him, "Ephphatha," that is, "Be opened."

Immediately his ears were opened, and the impediment [lit. *bond*] of his tongue was loosed, and he spoke plainly. (Mark 7:32–35)

The King James Version renders verse 35 as "and the string of his tongue was loosed."

If you and I are tongue-tied when it comes to speaking clearly to the lost about their salvation, it seems that, like the lingual frenulum in the boy, our conscience is falling short of what it should be doing. Let's loosen our tongues. Let's undergo a simple operation with the cutting words of Charles Spurgeon: "Have you no wish for others to be saved? Then you are not saved yourself. Be sure of that."[4]

If we say we are too shy and don't know what to say to the unsaved, we are more concerned about ourselves than we are about the eternal salvation of those who are heading for hell. How, then, can we think that God's love dwells in us? Such thoughts should put the fear of God into us, so that we go to the unsaved and speak clearly.[5]

In John 1, when the Pharisees asked John the Baptist seven probing questions, he wasn't tongue-tied. Each question was essentially asking for a reason for the hope that John had within him, and he answered them without hesitation. He said that the reason for his hope was the person of Jesus, the straps of whose sandals he wasn't worthy to untie. And John's purpose in existing was to be a voice in the wilderness to prepare the way for Him. He uncompromisingly plagued his hearers with the law and preached the sweetness of the gospel, as pictured in his diet of locusts and honey. He was a burning and shining light.

To be an effective evangelist, you must be loving, obedient, decisive, defiant, focused, prepared, truthful, practiced, faithful, and prayerful. I hope I've given you enough practical ways to live out these qualities and inspired you to evangelize. If you're having trouble getting started, start with prayer.

John never said, "Anyone but me." He was always ready. May we always be the same.

Notes

Chapter 1 Loving

1. Watch each of Jaclyn Glenn's reactions on video: Living Waters, *Crazy Bible* (2018), YouTube, accessed September 17, 2019, https://www.youtube.com/watch?v=z0-Q3Jl7vng&t=200s.

2. These gift cards are available through LivingWaters.com.

3. I'm not kidding! Read the whole article about golf spending here: Tim Parker, "Golf Clubs: When It Pays to Join One," Investopedia, updated March 17, 2016, https://www.investopedia.com/articles/wealth-management/031716/golf-clubs-when-it-pays-join-one.

Chapter 2 Obedient

1. "What Is the Meaning of the Greek Word *Dunamis* in the Bible?," Got Questions, accessed September 17, 2019, https://www.gotquestions.org/dunamis-meaning.html. I always find it helpful to look up the working definition of Greek words. The internet can help those of us who aren't full-time scholars. Sites like this one can help your own pursuits.

Chapter 3 Decisive

1. If you ever need to be reminded of the beauty of creation, see Signe Dean, "World's 7 Most Romantic Animals," *National Geographic*, February 14, 2017, https://www.nationalgeographic.com.au/animals/worlds-10-most-romantic-animals.aspx.

2. The entire article can be found here: Rabbi David Wolpe, "We Are Defining Love the Wrong Way," *Time*, February 16, 2016, http://time.com/4225777/meaning-of-love/.

Chapter 4 Defiant

1. To learn more about isolationism, see Susan Dunn, "The Debate behind U.S. Intervention in World War II," *The Atlantic*, July 8, 2013, https://www.the atlantic.com/national/archive/2013/07/the-debate-behind-us-intervention-in -world-war-ii/277572/.

2. Lexico, s.v. "redeem," accessed October 28, 2019, https://www.lexico.com /en/definition/redeem.

3. If you've never read any Wesley, this is a good place to start: "On Redeeming the Time," sermon 93, January 20, 1782, Wesley Center Online, accessed December 14, 2018, https://www.whdl.org/sites/default/files/publications/EN _John_Wesley_093_on_redeeming_time.htm.

4. Quoted in Wesley, "On Redeeming the Time."

Chapter 5 Focused

1. I find Barna studies to be reliable and effective. Here is the one about teenagers and their falling rates of faith: Samuel Smith, "Gen Z Is the Least Christian Generation in American History, Barna Finds," *Christian Post*, January 24, 2018, https://www.christianpost.com/news/gen-z-is-the-least-christian-generation-in -american-history-barna-finds.html.

2. Smith, "Gen Z Is the Least Christian Generation."

3. "The Story of God with . . . ," YouTube TV, accessed October 28, 2019, https://tv.youtube.com/browse/the-story-of-god-with-morgan-freeman-UCOB DtrLOytA4rwH5jTuIdLw.

4. This is where I found the episode: *The Story of God*, "Apocalypse," season 1, episode 2 (April 11, 2016), YouTube, accessed September 17, 2019, https://www .youtube.com/watch?v=yOuOqaDyTzk&list=ELhlWm36KZhtiUll0nRy5haQ.

Chapter 6 Prepared

1. Lexico, s.v. "crisis," accessed October 28, 2019, https://www.lexico.com /en/definition/crisis.

2. "Officials Release Video from Arizona Gender Reveal Party That Ignited a 47,000-Acre Wildfire," CNN, November 29, 2018, https://www.nbc15.com/con tent/news/Officials-release-video-from-Arizona-gender-reveal-party-that-ignit ed-a-47000-acre-wildfire-501541702.html.

3. I love Spurgeon. I find that accessing his material greatly enhances my morning quiet times. This one is from his devotional classic, *Morning and Evening*, May 26th—Evening Reading.

Chapter 7 Truthful

1. Dictionary.com, s.v. "gospel truth," accessed September 17, 2019, https:// www.dictionary.com/browse/gospel-truth.

2. Dictionary.com, s.v. "take as gospel," accessed September 17, 2019, https:// www.dictionary.com/browse/take-as-gospel.

3. Read the whole article here: Associated Press, "Suicide, at 50-Year Peak, Pushes Down US Life Expectancy," Newsmax, November 29, 2018, https://www .newsmax.com/newsfront/suicide-life-expectancy-peak/2018/11/29/id/892440/.

4. "Suicide, at 50-Year Peak."

5. Blue Letter Bible provides great resources for believers: C. H. Spurgeon, "Preach the Gospel," August 5, 1855, accessed September 17, 2019, https://www .blueletterbible.org/Comm/spurgeon_charles/sermons/0034.cfm.

Chapter 8 Practiced

1. C. H. Spurgeon, "The Perpetuity of the Law of God," May 21, 1882, Spurgeon Gems, accessed September 17, 2019, https://www.spurgeongems.org/vols 28-30/chs1660.pdf.

2. Spurgeon, "Preach the Gospel."

3. Michael Shear, Adam Goldman, and Emily Cochrane, "Congressman Steve Scalise Gravely Wounded in Alexandria Baseball Field Ambush," *New York Times*, June 14, 2017, https://www.nytimes.com/2017/06/14/us/steve-scalise-con gress-shot-alexandria-virginia.html.

4. Steve Scalise, "Floor Speech Marking Return to Congress Following the Congressional Baseball Shooting," delivered September 28, 2017, American Rhetoric, https://www.americanrhetoric.com/speeches/stevescaliseinjuryreturn housefloor.htm.

Chapter 9 Faithful

1. The entire elevator incident can be read about here: "Elevator at One of Chicago's Tallest Skyscrapers Plunges 84 Floors after Hoist Rope Breaks," *CBS News*, November 19, 2018, https://www.cbsnews.com/news/chicago-elevator-plunges -rescue-875-north-michigan-avenue-building-formerly-the-john-hancock-center/.

2. If you take nothing else from this book about sources for good material, remember C. H. Spurgeon. This is from his sermon "The Word a Sword," May 17, 1887, Spurgeon Gems, accessed September 17, 2019, https://www.spurgeon gems.org/vols34-36/chs2010.pdf.

3. For more from this great evangelist, start with this article: Greg Koukl, "A Stone in His Shoe," Stand to Reason, February 21, 2013, https://www.str.org/arti cles/a-stone-in-his-shoe.

Chapter 10 Prayerful

1. Read the entire sermon here: John MacArthur, "Understanding the Seducing Spirit," Grace to You, August 31, 1986, https://www.gty.org/library/sermons-li brary/54-29/understanding-the-seducing-spirit.

2. David Raksin Quote, IMDb, accessed September 17, 2109, https://m.imdb .com/name/nm0000710/quotes?ref_=m_nm_trv_trv.

3. Read more about Nick Hague here: Meghan Bartels, "NASA Astronaut Nick Hague 'Rolls with Punches' after Harrowing Soyuz Launch Failure," October

16, 2018, https://www.space.com/42155-soyuz-abort-astronaut-nick-hague-first
-interviews.html.

4. Paris Reidhead, *Getting Evangelicals Saved* (Bloomington, MN: Bethany House, 1989), n.p.

5. What follows is adapted from a video transcript.

6. Another great sermon from the Prince of Preachers: C. H. Spurgeon, "Pride the Destroyer," October 9, 1898, Spurgeon Gems, https://www.spurgeongems.org /vols43-45/chs2591.pdf.

7. Spurgeon, "Pride the Destroyer."

8. This is the full article about his suicide: John Updike, "A Case of Melancholia," *New Yorker*, February 12, 1989, https://www.newyorker.com/magazine /1989/02/20/a-case-of-melancholia.

9. John Wesley, "On Redeeming the Time," January 20, 1782, Rapture Ready, accessed September 17, 2019, https://www.raptureready.com/wesley-93/.

10. Read all the research here: Christoph Randler, "Defend Your Research: The Early Bird Really Does Get the Worm," *Harvard Business Review*, July–August 2010, https://hbr.org/2010/07/defend-your-research-the-early-bird-really-does -get-the-worm.

11. I found this Spurgeon quote here: "Soul Winning," Christian Classics Ethereal Library, accessed September 17, 2019, https://www.ccel.org/ccel/spur geon/proverbs.xii.html.

12. Spurgeon, "Soul Winning."

13. These and other items are available from LivingWaters.com.

Final Thoughts

1. Read more about ignorance as a lack of excuse here: Thomas Seigel, "Ignorance of the Law May Be an Excuse," Lawyers.com, accessed September 17, 2019, https://www.lawyers.com/legal-info/research/ignorance-of-the-law-may -be-an-excuse.html.

2. Seigel, "Ignorance of the Law."

3. John Bunyan, *The Pilgrim's Progress*, 1678 ed. (CreateSpace Independent Publishing, 2015), 10.

4. C. H. Spurgeon, "She Was Not Hid," April 15, 1888, Spurgeon Gems, accessed September 17, 2019, https://www.spurgeongems.org/vols34-36/chs2019 .pdf.

5. LivingWaters.com exists to help you overcome your fears and fulfill the Great Commission. We even have tracts that are designed (for wimps like me) to provide plenty of get-away time. You can give one to a cashier or leave one for a waiter and you will be long gone before they even discover it's a gospel tract. Better to give and run than not to give at all.

Ray Comfort is the cohost (with Kirk Cameron) of the award-winning television program *Way of the Master*. He is the founder of Living Waters Publications and is dedicated to equipping Christians with resources to fulfill the Great Commission. Ray is the bestselling author of more than ninety books, including *The Evidence Bible*, a Christian Book Award finalist. He has written for Billy Graham's *Decision* magazine, and his literature is used by the Moody Bible Institute, Leighton Ford Ministries, Campus Crusade for Christ, and the Institute for Scientific and Biblical Research. Ray and his wife, Sue, live in Southern California and have three grown children.

FOR ANYONE WHO WANTS TO
SHARE THE GOSPEL EFFECTIVELY

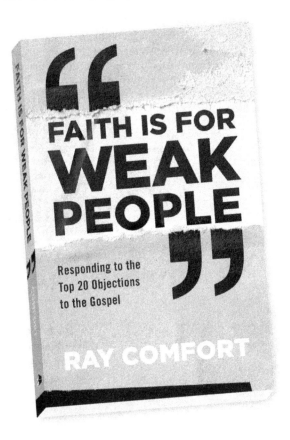

We are in a battle. At stake? The souls of our friends, family members, and coworkers.

Apologist and evangelist Ray Comfort has spent his entire career sharing the faith and answering people's objections to it. He wants you to be equipped to do the same. In this practical book, he shows you how to answer twenty objections to Christianity.

Don't go into battle unarmed. Let Ray Comfort train you to be ready with an answer— not so you can be right, but so you can help bring people from darkness into light.

LIVING WATERS

RAY COMFORT is the CEO/founder of Living Waters. Living Waters exists to inspire and equip Christians to fulfill the Great Commission. Like many believers, you may be hesitant to share the gospel with your unbelieving friends and family for fear of causing offense. If the thought of sharing your faith terrifies you, you're not alone. Living Waters has wonderful resources that will help you overcome your fears and reach those you love.

READ, WATCH, LISTEN
LivingWaters.com offers a host of equipping and encouraging material you can enjoy anytime, with new content added daily.

UNIQUE GOSPEL TRACTS
These tracts are so interesting that unbelievers will ask you for more. Sharing the gospel has never been easier.

AWARD-WINNING TV SHOW & MOVIES
From evolution and atheism to one-on-one witnessing and apologetics, a wide variety of free videos are available online.

Learn more at **LivingWaters.com**

KEEP UP WITH
RAY and HIS MINISTRY

LIVING WATERS publishes daily witnessing clips on YouTube (over 100,000,000 views). Watching these will help to equip you to share your faith.

LIVINGWATERS.COM

 RayComfort // LivingWatersPub

Living Waters

official.Ray.Comfort

LIKE THIS
BOOK?
Consider sharing it with others!

- Share or mention the book on your social media platforms. Use the hashtag **#AnyoneButMe**.

- Write a book review on your blog or on a retailer site.

- Pick up a copy for friends, family, or anyone who you think would enjoy and be challenged by its message!

- Share this message on Twitter, Facebook, or Instagram: **I loved #AnyoneButMe by @RayComfort // @ReadBakerBooks**

- Recommend this book for your church, workplace, book club, or class.

- Follow Baker Books on social media and tell us what you like.

 ReadBakerBooks

 ReadBakerBooks

 ReadBakerBooks